Diary of a
Freedom
Writer

GW00503779

CO-AUTHOR OF THE *NEW YORK TIMES* BESTSELLING BOOK *FREEDOM WRITERS DIARY*

Diary of a Freedom Writer

The Experience

DARRIUS GARRETT

TATE PUBLISHING
AND ENTERPRISES, LLC

Published by Tate Publishing & Enterprises, LLC
127 E. Trade Center Terrace | Mustang, Oklahoma 73064 USA
1.888.361.9473 | www.tatepublishing.com

Tate Publishing is committed to excellence in the publishing industry. The company reflects the philosophy established by the founders, based on Psalm 68:11,
"The Lord gave the word and great was the company of those who published it."

Published in the United States of America

ISBN: 978-1-62563-580-8
1. Biography & Autobiography / Personal Memoirs
2. Biography & Autobiography / General
13.04.25

Dedication

To my dearest mother,

The day I was created, I was placed in your womb. When born, I was placed in your arms. When I was homeless, I was on your mind. But when I became a man, I was on your heart. The reason I say this is because all my life you carried me. And now, since you're gone, I'm carrying you… right here in my heart, mind, and soul. I love you, Mom, and I spent most of our time together on this earth trying to make you proud.

Becoming a success was my tool that I wanted to use to put that smile on your face and that house in your name. I guess what I'm saying is, my sadness isn't in seeing you die; my sadness is in not seeing you live… because you dedicated your life to us…your children. You gave a lot for us as there are many things that I wish you would have gotten the opportunity to do. I wanted to make that happen, but I guess at some point, as most of us will do, we just ran out of time.

That's why I work so hard and diligently to finish things. I never want to feel that feeling of running out of time again.

I have three little girls now, and there is something in each and every one of them that reminds me of you. I have to laugh sometimes because it seems like now I'm your father because of how closely their personalities match yours. Beyond anything, Mom, I hope I make you proud at some point before my journey ends.

I decided to release this book and dedicate it to you on April 21, your birthday. I never got to do the things I wanted to do for you, so in some way I hope that you are able to get word of this dedication from your fellow angels that are keeping you company. I hope you continue to live through me, and I pray we can enjoy the perks of success together. It was my dream to do something for you, society, and my generation. With Diary of A Freedom Writer, my dream has come true. I dedicate this book to my mother, Marie Garrett, a woman who gave all and asked for nothing....Happy birthday, Mom.

Marie Garrett
April 21, 1944–May 7, 2010

Acknowledgments

I am so appreciative to all who helped me in this process of releasing this book and making a dream come true. I want to first of all thank God, the fans, people who continued to believe, and never doubted in their minds that this would happen. People like Julie Sanders from Oregon. I want to thank some key ladies such as my late mother Marie Garrett for being the strong woman that she is, sister Patrice Perkins for being a second mother in my life, my wife Jamia Garrett for staying in my corner while I fight in the ring against life and all other adversaries, my daughters Sarye, Aaliyah, and Reagan Garrett for keeping me alive, as well as the newest addition to our family, Jalen Garrett. If it was not for my daughters, I probably would have lost all hope. Caliste Coffey for being a key believer in my life and always being an ear for my problems and giving sound and loving advice. The Freedom Writer Family/ Foundation as a whole helped mold me into the writer I have become and the man I needed to be, and Ms. Gruwell, my mentor, as she helped mold me and place me into the position I was destined to be in as a man, actor, writer, speaker, and most of all as a father.

I want to go down the list of men in my life that may have or have not been mentioned in this composition but played a key role in my development, such as: Edward Garrett Jr. (brother), Darryl Little (brother), Larry Clark Sr. (uncle), Brother Newman (godfather), Johnny Perkins (brother-in-law), Elder Clifton Edwards Sr. (counselor when father died/childhood pastor), Dean Kinsey (Middle School Dean), Donnell Little (uncle), Mr. Crawford (8th grade teacher/introduced me to football), Dr. Pieter Van Neil (Acting Theatre Teacher), Coach David Slaney (football coach), Mr. Hall (HS Gov. teacher), Coach Alpizar (Track & Field Coach/Spanish Teacher), late Mr. Steve Gruwell aka "Papa G" (Ms. Gruwell's dad), Chris Gruwell (Ms. Gruwell's brother, dear friend, and helper to the Freedom Writers), Keron Jones (best friend), Henry Jones (best friend), Narada Comans (best friend), Steven Moore (best friend), Stephen Kendrick (best friend), Harold Cofer Jr. (best friend), Antoine Benson (best friend), Billy Wingfield (best friend), Mr. Shelton (Middle School PE Teacher), Mr. White (Middle School PE Teacher), Mr. Hill aka Big Daddy (College Admin/Mentor), Pastor Thomas Alexander Sr. (Pastor), Mr. George (freedom writer George Ryan's dad), all my brothers within the Freedom Writers, Mr. Avery (mentor), Adrian & Roko Belic (friends), Richard Brinson (mentor), Ronald Garrett (father-in-law), Jacob Cottrell (friend), and someone who treated all the Freedom Writer men like sons, Don Parris (mentor/father figure). I thank you and love you all for your contributions to my life.

Though the men previously mentioned seemed to be many, the truth is for the jobs that they all contributed together within me to do, it only took one who could have done it all if he had made the right decision to do so—my father.

Edward Garrett Sr.
October 9th, 1947–January 17, 1993

"Men, be a father to your children. Your presence is greatly needed."

When speaking at events such as schools, conferences, churches, and other events, I currently utilize *Diary of a Freedom Writer: The Experience* as a teaching tool to help others find a way. I hope you will do the same by sharing this book with those that you love as well as invite me to speak at your next event. We are all in this together as the next book will probably be about you or your students.

God Bless.

—Darrius Garrett

Pay Darrius a visit via social network

www.Darriusonline.com
www.twitter.com/herbanprince
www.linkedin.com/in/darriusgarrett/
www.facebook.com/DiaryOfAFreedomWriter
www.facebook.com/pages/Darrius-Garrett/
319980318095610

Table of Contents

Foreword

by Erin Gruwell

As an English teacher, I learned from my students, like Darrius Garrett, that everyone has a story. And more important, great storytellers don't always have to leap from the pages of textbooks like Shakespeare or Homer (or as Darrius once referred to them as "dead white guys in tights"). Everyone has a story—even a troubled teenager who walked into my classroom with a rap sheet, but more impressively, walked out with a diploma.

My introduction to Darrius Garret was when a disgruntled colleague handed me a thick manila envelope in the teacher's lounge with Darrius's name scribbled on the tab and a flippant comment like, "Read it and weep!" My heart sunk. As a new teacher, I was given the students that no one else wanted— those who had just come out of juvenile hall, or were recently released from rehab, and all the disciplinary transfers who were suspended from other schools. I hesitated for a moment and then decided not to open the folder and read its contents. I didn't want to know what was in that folder. Concerned looks from my colleagues followed. They couldn't believe that I didn't devour the fine print. Didn't I want to know about his record? Wasn't I remotely curious about his stint in juvenile hall? Why did he transfer to Wilson High? How bad were his test scores? My colleagues believed that Darrius was destined to fail, and they couldn't understand why I didn't want to be forewarned about all the labels that were bestowed upon him. Early on in my teaching career, I had decided that students like Darrius were more than just a number branded on their uniform, more than the statistics associated with their color or creed, and certainly more than a test score. So rather than read what other people had written about Darrius, I decided that he would write what needed to be written, tell what needed to be told. Even though Darrius couldn't change his past or the content of that manila folder, I remained hopeful that he could write volumes about his future.

And thus, Darrius's literary journey began.

By the time Darrius had walked into my classroom, he had already buried dozens of friends to senseless gang violence. He had watched his friends get gunned down on street corners, he had visited relatives behind bars, and he had buried his father to AIDS. I wondered if Darrius could write about this cast of characters and learn how not to repeat their tragic fate. Darrius had claimed that he lived in "an undeclared war," and for that reason I wanted to encourage him to put down his gun and pick up a pen. I wanted Darrius to tell his story with the same bravado as Shakespeare writing about Hamlet, or Homer writing about Odysseus. Each of these literary protagonists had overcome huge obstacles and inspired readers with their heroism in the face of grave danger and their courage in confronting their nemeses. While Darrius would not have to stand up to kings and sirens like his imaginary counterparts, he would, in fact, have to dodge kingpins who ruled his streets, or cover his ears to block out the shrill of cop sirens barreling down his block.

I assigned Darrius and his fellow classmates books written by, for, and about kids who also had equally powerful stories to tell. Stories about looking out a tiny little attic, like Anne Frank, or riding in a cattle car into a concentration camp, like Elie Wiesel, or even dodging sniper bullets on the streets of Sarajevo, like Zlata Filipovic. Each of these gripping stories, written by teenagers in the middle of genocide, told tales about fighting back with words rather than with weapons. I hoped that my students could fight the urban genocide proliferated on the streets of Long Beach with words, rather than rely on semi-automatic weapons.

Through lessons learned from these fearless young writers, my hope was that Darrius would find his voice, and that Darrius would record his story.

In addition to young authors like Anne Frank, I shared with my students other genres of writing and wise writers who were able to reach the masses. We devoured Alice Walker and her Pulitzer prized winning book, *The Color Purple*. We debated Maya Angelou's *I Know Why the Caged Bird Sings*. We dared to compare Tupac Shakur's "A Rose in Concrete" to life in Long Beach. And we wrestled to understand Langston Hughes' "A Dream Deferred."

In honor of these sages, students like Darrius began to write—essays, poems, short stories—and boldly dubbed themselves the Freedom Writers, in homage of the Civil Rights Activists, Freedom Riders. The Freedom Riders fought segregation in our country, and in essence, were able to fight the good fight. The result of their movement is that the Freedom Riders changed the ugly practice of segregation in our country. As my students began to write, they too had the desire to fight the good fight—to fight misconceptions, to fight stereotypes, and to fight the bias in our educational system. They wanted people to know that kids who look like Darrius, talk like Darrius, and come from a place where Darrius comes from are more than just a number, more than a rap sheet, and more than a test score.

After graduation from high school, my students were able to compile their stories in a book, *The Freedom Writers Diary*, and share their four-year journey in Room 203 with the world. None of them expected the book would have the impact that it did—especially the profound impact their words had on kids and their teachers. Suddenly teachers were able to see their students in a different light, and kids were inspired to write their own stories. They, too, could write their own ending.

Once the Freedom Writers graduated, and I could no longer assign them essays to write or authors to read, my hope was that they would realize that their story wasn't over, and that the literary journey would still continue. Unfortunately, for young men like Darrius, one chapter ended, and another one began. Without the comfort and safety of Room 203, Darrius had to navigate the seas of adulthood in the same way that Odysseus sailed the treacherous seas in *The Odyssey*. In some cases, the sea was equally as rough, equally as challenging.

Even though Darrius no longer had to worry about Number Two pencils or my latest pop quiz, he would have other tests to pass. What did it mean to be a man, when there was no man in his house to guide him? What did it mean to be a husband, when there was no example for him to reference? What did it mean to provide for his family, when the lessons he learned as a child were heartbreaking? While Darrius was no longer dodging bullets on the streets or being chased by the law, the challenges were just as tough. As a teenager, he had less to lose, but as an adult, he now had a farther fall from grace, and the consequences were more extreme.

Since Darrius and his cohorts chronicled their story in *The Freedom Writers Diary*, the art of writing has changed. When students like Darrius began the writing process, they did not have computers in their homes, smart phones in their pockets, and a Facebook account at their fingertips. The immediacy of the written word had not yet gone viral, and the impact of social media was yet to be experienced. But with this newfound immediacy, one questions: how are words used, and what are they used for? How does one tell his or her story? In a post or in a tweet? Thus, as a passionate English teacher who began her career with books, I am elated that Darrius chose the medium of a book to share his story. Hopefully his book can get in the hands of a young boy who is trying to find his voice, or a teenager searching for redemption behind bars, or a man trying to navigate his way through adulthood.

Darrius Garrett's story is a journey of heartbreak and heroism, courage and conviction, and the noble attempt to write the wrong. May his story encourage you, the reader, to pick up your own pen and write your own story.

Preface

I recall a great writer/critic named Lawrence Clark quoted saying, "Write to be understood, speak to be heard, read to grow." As I wrote this book, I did just that. Since 1999, when the *Freedom Writers* book was released, we had a voice, but there was no face to the voices. Then in 2007, when the *Freedom Writers* movie debuted, we had a face put to the voice, but the faces weren't ours. I was inspired to write this book because I would travel and speak to schools, juvenile facilities, churches, and arenas as people would ask the same questions of my background before I became a freedom writer. Instead of answering those questions individually, I decided to answer them in this book as well as do something that has not been done, take you home with a freedom writer, placing you, the reader into the passenger seat of my life, from the adolescent age of nine until reaching adulthood.

The book we as freedom writers wrote as kids tells our individual stories in the past, and the movie tells the freedom writer story as a whole, but *Diary of a Freedom Writer: The Experience* will give you a first person's eye view of what I went through to get there, the process of change, as well as stories of the encounters that catapulted the freedom writers to the level of success that we have reached in our lives today. My hope is that you will find this book educational, interesting, and maybe even funny at times. As a child, teen, and adult, I have encountered a lot in this small space in time and lived to write about it. I ask that you share this book with your husband, wife, son, daughter, niece, nephew, brother, sister, students, or anyone who can learn from my story. Pass it on to others to help them possibly encounter change and live a better quality life. I realize that I am called to utilize my experiences to help others and I expect this book to do just that. I believe there is something in this book for everyone from the gangster who feels hopeless to the college student trying to figure out the rest of his life. My hope is that *Diary of a Freedom Writer: The Experience* will uplift, educate, encourage, as well as inspire.

Born to Live, Bred to Die

Constantly waking up to the sound of bullets ringing out in the alleyway outside my second-story apartment window made me numb to the reality of violence and death as a kid. I never thought that my life was any different from anyone else's. My thoughts were that we lived in the same type of environment and in fear all over the world. Things had gotten so bad at one point that when you heard a gunshot, you could tell where it came from, but if you were really good, you could tell what type of gun was fired. People from my neighborhood were so accustomed to this lifestyle that it wasn't shocking or scary to hear a gun go off or to find out that someone had been shot or killed. It just felt like we were children growing up during a war, an undeclared war.

At the age of nine, I recall walking outside the front door of our small yellow apartment to see my neighbor's granddaughter being beat up by these guys. She was taking one blow after another, being kicked, hit, and stomped on over and over. Even though I was only nine years old, I wanted to run out there and do something to help her. Exposure to this act of violence made my heart race and my adrenaline pump, yet all I could do was watch. As they stopped, she got up, and blood was coming out of her mouth and nose. But the craziest thing happened after: they all gave her hugs and embraced her.

Later as I grew up, I found out she was getting "put on the set" (*being initiated into a gang*). That particular situation became oh so familiar when I would go to Martin Luther King Park, located on the Eastside of Long Beach, California. I saw guys and girls alike getting put on all the time. Sometimes, it was funny to me and my friends because it was entertaining to watch people get beat up. Yet it was preparing us for our time to come. We were like soldiers in training. I guess you could say I always thought as a leader. I never let anyone persuade me to do something I had not already thought about doing anyway. I always voiced that I would never let anybody beat me up to be part of a click, crew, or gang; if anything, I'm a benefit to them. So why did I have to pay with my face being kicked in? The way it was explained to me is that you show you have heart. When you get put on the set, that's showing you are not a punk, which displays your heart and passion to be part of that gang.

There was always something happening every other day in the streets. My friends and I were finally figuring out what neighborhood we were going to be from. Usually, the average thirteen-year-old would consider that an important age because that is the time their bodies are changing or the age that they are transitioning from a preteen to an actual teenager, but not me or my friends.

There were only two major black gangs in my neighborhood, the Rollin 20's Crips and the Insane Crips. Be it that I grew up in an environment that is dominated by gangs that are of the Crips organization,

I often heard the greeting term "cuzz" (a term used to greet a fellow crip gang member) a lot. My neighborhood was sectioned into an L shape where one gang was on one section of the L and the other gang on the other section of the L and everyone who grew up there knew that line. When my friends and I became of age, it was destined for us to be from one hood or the other. The same group of boys that once played cowboys and Indians when we were younger are now playing modern-day cowboys and Indians as they became bitter enemies, killing up one another.

The saddest part of the situation is if one gang member had a problem with someone from the other gang, then every member of the initial gang had a problem with the members of the rival gang regardless of who they were. I recall a story told to me by my brother Ed about cousins who grew up in my neighborhood that were from these two rival gangs, one was from the Rollin 20's Crips gang and the other cousin was from the Insane Crips gang. The two gangs had a problem with each other, which was the onset of a gang war. The cousins wound up killing each other for their turf and their beef (slang term used for a problem amongst two people or entities). Yeah, that deep!

One thing I learned a lot about living in Long Beach, California, was loyalty. It was the type of loyalty that would cause you to never snitch on your enemy. It was a loyalty to the streets. An unwritten code of ethics that all people in the hood just knew. Growing up, my father explained to me that from the street point of view, the situation will be handled, but you don't want to ever allow the police to be involved because the police are everyone's enemy. My dad would say, "Nobody likes a rat. A rat is considered as the lowest of the low and just like a rat; they will do whatever for the cheese, but when going for the cheese that the cops are dangling whether it's less time served or a 'fake get out of jail free' card, it winds up being a trap to get everyone caught, including you." I was told that if I was the kind of person that tells, then that's what I am: a rat. And nobody likes a rat.

I was a nice kid with a big heart and dreams. I was religiously raised, loved my family, and unconditionally loved my father, but after growing up with teachings like that, it forced me to hold a lot of things inside. The pain and hurt that I felt from different things that occurred in my life consumed me as I grew older. Slowly but surely, I was transforming from a good kid to a thug. The things that I felt and had bottled up inside needed to be released somehow. I began fighting all the time, thus bringing forth the death of an innocent little boy. See, being around my friends and my brother made the gang life not seem so bad.

Until one day, I was hanging out with my brother and his crew on Lewis Street. It was cool at the time because everyone was enjoying themselves, smoking, drinking, and slap-boxing in the street, just an all-around good summer day in the hood until a white Monte Carlo pulled up. Honestly, from that point, things became a blur as I saw the car roll up and some words were exchanged, and as soon as I glanced back at the car, all I saw was a .45 pointed our way. If it wasn't a .45, it was some *Dirty Harry*–looking gun.

My brother yelled, "Get down!" I was stuck. I couldn't move. Everything seemed to happen in slow motion; one shot rang out, then two, then three, four, and five. I guess you can say God was on my side that day because no bullets hit me. But my brothers' friend wasn't so fortunate. A girl screamed, and all I saw was a line of blood coming from where the body was as my brother and his homeboys were huddled around him, yelling for someone to call an ambulance. I don't know if I passed out from the witnessing of my first possible murder or what, but from that point of the story my memory of this incident became dark.

I will never forget that day. I was introduced to what really happens to gang members as well as innocent bystanders in the hood, and it formally introduced me to the gang life. My brother always glorified it, but he never wanted me to do it. He told me to stick to my Cross Colours jeans and Nintendo video games. I always wanted to be like him or my father. If that's what it took, being shot at, ducking bullets, putting in work to have my father or father figure in my life, then so be it. I was ready.

No Justice, No Peace

Growing up, my older brother Ed used to listen to NWA a lot before we went to sleep. At that time, I completely understood what was being said in their music because I would watch men on the streets be beaten by police officers daily in my neighborhood. One time, my mother told me a story about how a family friend was locked up and the police hung him in his jail cell but tried to make it seem like a suicide. My brother told me a story of how he was taken to jail, after being booked he was taken to his cell. The police pressed a button on the elevator, stopping it in between floors and he was beaten by the police. The men in my family with the last name Garrett was infamous to the LBPD due to my dad's retaliation against the police by beating one up. Given this history of police brutality against a lot of men from my neighborhood and other rural areas, it was evident that retaliation was soon to come.

The time was 1992. I had arrived home from school and saw on the news that this man named Rodney King had been beaten and the cops responsible were on trial. As I was trying to watch cartoons, the news flashed across the screen that the cops were found not guilty! Everyone was extremely upset, yet once again, the police department had gotten away with something that had been done to my family as well as my friend's families for so many years. As soon as the news came on to talk about what had happened, I heard a big crash and glass breaking. The war had begun. The things that I heard talked about as far as revolution and justice in the rap songs had started.

I ran outside, stood on the front porch, and all I could see was a black ball of smoke going into the air from a distance. I began to get scared as I did not understand what was going on. I didn't know if this was retaliation or just the demise of our whole neighborhood. As my mother and I watched television, I began to see the violence that went on in the streets of Los Angeles. People were being pulled out of cars, beaten, and dragged into the middle of the streets. I never saw so much violence happen at one time. On the other hand, I never seen so much unity among black people either; except for the Civil Rights Movement. The more I watched, the more I understood. I began to feel the anger and rage that was built in us from so many years and became upset as I realized what it all meant. Imagine being legally picked on, profiled, and beat on simply because someone didn't like you. Imagine being bullied and there is no one to tell because the ones you are supposed to tell are the ones doing the bullying. That is what this riot was all about, a group of people saying, "No More."

As the days grew, rioting and looting happened more and more. I remember my brother Ed coming to our mother's house with some brand-new rims and car audio stuff. When I went to school, my friends would talk about how their brothers got all these new things. So I began to think of the riots as an opportunity to get what I wanted. My friends came around and told me to join them as they went looting like we were going trick or treating.

I began to formulate my own opinions and justify the slogan that had been put out by the group NWA by saying, "Fuck the police!" I was ready to go with my friends and do just as my brother had done and take what I wanted. But one person stood in the way, my mother. Things got worse before they got better. Riding down the street with my mother and seeing burned-down buildings that had been in our neighborhood for years made me feel bad about my justifications of violence and looting in our community. I saw a Hispanic business owner and his wife out front with a bat trying to protect the only thing they had worked so hard for to support their family, and it was being burned to the ground in a matter of minutes along with other family-owned businesses as well. One of them being the store my mother frequented so much called Hanson's Market.

I also remember riding down by the school that my brother attended, Poly High, and seeing guys in military uniform with an MP (Military Police) sleeve on their arms. I began to see angry mobs still walking the streets, screaming the words, "No justice, no peace!" The aftermath of the riots in my Long Beach city neighborhood had now matched the look and likeness of a war torn country. Now, be it that I looked like the other people in the angry mob, and maybe even thought like them, there was something different about the situation that made me feel that even I was not safe in that environment. As the violence and anger in my neighborhood decreased, the healing began. The community joined together to help rebuild some of the places that were burned down. Yet the store my mother frequented (Hanson's) never returned. Which left the people in my neighborhood with less than what we had before this whole riot began. As I climbed into my bed, I thought of all that occurred. Yet all that mattered to me was that this nightmare would soon all be over.

Summer Madness

Summer of 1992 had finally arrived. I was already stricken by the death of my friend, Smurf, who had previously died from self-inflicted gunshot wounds after taking his brothers gun and trying to carry it for protection and power. The situation occurred when we were hanging out on that block. He tried to use the gun to scare someone. He tried to pull the gun, and I went to stop him. But he refused to hand the gun to me. I grabbed the gun and we began to tussle with each other, and a struggle began between us. I honestly thought that the gun wasn't loaded. If I had known that it was loaded then I would have never approached him. When I tried to snatch the gun or at least push it out of his hand, I don't know if he was trying to shoot me, but as the tussle continued I heard a loud bang; or I would say more like a loud *pow* type of noise.

A weird burn smell filled my nose. People scattered and ran while ducking. I saw blood running to the ground like water from a half-turned-on faucet. I knew I had been shot, at least until Smurf fell to the ground. Though I felt anxiety and fear like my throat was closing cutting off my air, I couldn't do anything but watch as he laid there gasping for air. I stayed with him until the police and ambulance came. His breathing became rapid then delayed. His body was fighting and his legs kicking, fighting for life until one last exhale escaped his little body and he died right in front of me.

That situation made me numb to death. I became very distant and dark. I wanted to be alone most of the time because it was hard to process what I had seen. I tried to talk to my mother about it, but she would disregard it like it didn't happen or I was lying. I heard before that once you encounter death it becomes easier, but for me it just got harder and my summer of madness had just begun. My next encounter with death was later that same summer. Troy, a friend of mine, and I were enrolled in summer school on the north side of Long Beach. I knew from experience that it would not be good to try and perpetrate that I was from any gang or neighborhood when I really wasn't. Though my friends had already made a decision of where they were going to be from, I didn't as I knew my brother and my father weren't going to let me be part of the gang anyway until I was of age to really make my own decision to be from the gang.

Troy wasn't as fortunate to have such caring relatives and he wasn't as wise either. The time was about 1:30pm as the bell rang, and we were gathering our things to leave class. I asked him what we were going to do that day. Our usual routine was to go to the local park and have lunch and try to mess around with the girls who were in the area. This day was a little different as we both decided that we were going to go home. As we sat on the bus stop, a car drove up and slowed down as they passed us. For some reason they were mad dogging (*staring to intimidate*) us. I had the feeling that there would be trouble as my brother had prepared me for situations like this; he let me know that "when that happens have your heat ready, because somebody is about to get shot." Unfortunately, I was not armed, nor was Troy.

Troy decided to hit the guys up with the gang sign that he'd seen our brothers throwing up to represent the hood. Then the car sped off as if he held up a shield or something that scared them, or so I thought. As we sat there, I thought for a minute how stupid that was to represent a gang that we're not even from yet. So I asked him, "Troy, why the f— you doing stupid s— like that man?"

"Awww. They ain't s—, cuz. Just some fake gangsters. They know who run this city."

After he said that, I began to think he knew what he was talking about because nobody came back. But one thing stuck out to me. If it wasn't a problem, then why did they speed off like that? A few minutes later I spotted the same car coming down the street.

My heart started to beat fast as my wisdom advised me that this wasn't going to end well. "Look, Troy...the same car," I said. "We might have to run. If we do, we just have to cut through the park and run back to the school, okay?"

"S—, I ain't running from nobody," he said. "This our hood."

I shook my head in disbelief to how oblivious to the possibilities of being shot Troy was as they rolled up. "What's up, cuzz," the guy in the passenger side of the car said as I nodded my head, gesturing *what's up* back to them.

Troy said, "What's up?" The dude in the passenger seat had his hands outside the car so I thought it was cool. But something seemed weird about the guy in the back. He was looking around like he was making sure the coast was clear to rob us or something. "Hey, cuzz, where the weed at?" the man in the car said. I shrugged and shook my head, not saying a word letting them know I didn't know.

Troy decided to have an all out conversation with them. The guy then says, "Hey, come here real quick, lil cuzz." I stayed behind when Troy walked up to the car. The guy in the back asked, "Don't I know you?" And troy responded saying, "I don't know…probably." The guy then asked the infamous question, "Where y'all from?" Troy responded with the name of the local gang in our area. As the guy looked like he was grabbing for something in front of him, he pulled a gun saying, "F— crabs" (a derogatory term for a Crips gang member). Once again things seem to happen in slow motion as I ran to the park we agreed to run into. I ran so hard that I dropped my bag and everything, not noticing if Troy was running with me. When I got to the park, I looked around and noticed that Troy followed closely behind as we ran across the street into this park. The car sped off and we stopped to catch our breath. As we were walking, Troy all of a sudden remembered he had an aunt who lived down the street and he could go to her house for a little while, leaving me to have to go home alone. I know he was scared, but so was I.

From that point on, I learned about friendship and the lack thereof. As I walked to the bus stop, I could hear my mother saying, "Darrius, you don't have friends, you have associates." I went back to the same bus stop we almost got shot at because I was not going to walk all the way down the street almost five blocks while risking myself getting shot at when I could catch the bus right here. As I transcended from deep thought, the bus pulled right up. Talk about a miracle. When I got on the bus, I heard about six to eight gunshots in the distance. From that point I knew what had happened. When I got home, I called Troy and there was no answer. I called back to back, but still...no answer.

The weekend passed and Monday arrived. Troy did not come to class. Everyone began talking about a kid getting shot down the street from the park next door last Friday. It was Troy...another human being now not living anymore. The saddest part of the whole scenario was that the guy sitting in the back of the car did know Troy. He and Troy played Pop Warner football as kids together when Troy stayed with his grandmother in Compton. They were on the same football team. Now Troy is dead and the other guy is in jail for life. I began to think to myself, *How many more times do I have to go through this? Am I next?* Such were the thoughts wandering like lost, scattered sheep in my mind. I wouldn't have doubted if I was the next one to die. I was only twelve going on thirteen, and I couldn't stand to have to bury someone else. At this rate, I knew my day was coming soon. Most people have fond memories of their summers because of all the fun they had. I share the same feelings of memories of my summers, but not because of all the fun I had. But because of the friends I buried this time of season every other year of the season I call summer madness.

Where's My Father?

Where was my father? That was the million-dollar question asked by millions of children in the hood. I spent all my life trying to have a relationship with my dad. Though often absent; I loved my father dearly. For what it's worth, at least I can say that I knew him and he knew who I was. My father has been in and out of prison for most of my life. I can't recall more than ten times that I have encountered my father without him eventually going to jail or just getting out of jail. I always had faith in him that one day he would turn it all around and become the model citizen that I would lie to my friends about him being. I recall a time as early as kindergarten and the kids would talk about how their fathers would take them to baseball games and on their jobs in the various professions in which the fathers worked, like being lawyers, doctors, and athletes.

Since I knew that my father didn't fit any of those criteria to be in those professions or had a job like their dads, I began to create this person in my mind that I thought of to be my father. A fighter pilot, tall and handsome. A ladies' man yet only committed to my mother and a personality mix of Martin, Malcolm, and Gandhi. But it couldn't have been so far from the truth. My mother would tell me that for some reason, I just had some kind of connection with him. She used to always tell me this story of us going to visit him in the state penitentiary when I was only two years old. She said that he was coming out on the line chained to a group of other inmates, and little old me—this short, stubby, two-year-old—pointed in his direction and screamed, "There's my daddy." I hobbled past all the other inmates with my short little legs only to run to him. So I guess you could say that he and I always had a connection.

It isn't that my father was a really bad man. He just made bad decisions. As a kid, I loved my father because although he wasn't the tall tale male that I bragged about to friends in school, I loved him dearly. Though he didn't finish high school and he made bad decisions, I personally felt that my dad and my brother had greatness within them, and I firmly believed that until the day they both died. They never allowed that greatness to surface. At times I felt cursed by carrying my fathers' last name. On the other hand, also deep down inside, I felt a royal lineage by being my father's son, like the lion king with Simba and his father Mufasa. Though the things he taught me weren't of how to be a man but of how to survive in the streets, just as Mufasa taught Simba how to pounce. Both teachings resulted the same outcome—*survival*. I wish my dad had taught me more about life like how to love, treat a woman, and take care of family. But growing up and maturing allowed me to ask the question, *How can one teach something they have not mastered themselves?*

It was late 1992, and my last visit with my father and speaking to him was in jail. He had finally come to terms that he had full-blown AIDS, and he wanted to share that information with me. I went to talk to him, and he just started apologizing to me. From a twelve-year-old perspective, I was thinking he was apologizing for not being there or for the times he promised me he was going to pick me up and I was left standing on the porch waiting for him. I will never forget times like that, because when I think of those moments, I envision myself as a little kid with my backpack full of clothes in one hand and my brother's old electronic football game in the other, waiting on the porch until the sun set and the streetlights came on because he never showed up and my mother left there to clean up the specs of hurt and pain left on that porch from his lies time and time again.

I thought he was apologizing for that. But no, he was apologizing because he had full-blown AIDS. Now at that time, he had gotten the disease when it was considered or referred to by people in my community as a disease that only struck gay men, but he actually acquired it from sharing needles. All this time he was worried about me thinking that he's gay. I couldn't care less about his sexual orientation. I only cared about his fatherly duties to me. I didn't understand at the time, but I had gotten really upset as I thought to myself, *Wow, he's not apologizing for not being a father and being there for me or for the times he left me stranded on that porch, but he actually is trying to defend his manhood.*

Through it all, I realized my love for him and accepted his apology. He promised that things have changed, and when he gets out of jail, he is going to do his best to be the father that he has not been in the past. It was so refreshing to hear.

I saw this as a second chance with me, his son, a boy that has wanted his father in his life for the last twelve to thirteen years. A few months later, my dad was released from prison. I held on to his promise. Every night before I went to sleep I would replay that time in prison before I left when he bent down and looked me in the eye and promised that he's going to be as much of a father to me as he could with the time he has left and gracefully fall asleep with a big smile on my face.

Fatherless Child

January 1993 had come, my father had thrown a New Year's gathering at his house. My mom didn't allow me to go because I had messed up in school. I begged my mother, but she still didn't allow me to attend. Weeks later, I was woken up out of my sleep to my mother saying, "Darrius, your father is in the hospital, he was hospitalized with pneumonia and he only has an hour to live; your dad is about to die" I felt it in my mind and body that something was wrong already before my mother said it. The day I was invited to the New Year's party, I felt that would be the last time I seen my dad if I was able to go. As we got to the hospital, family was gathered around, the clergy had everyone gathered in this room, and he just kept saying, "Let's pray." While the clergy was trying to get everyone to pray, I was trying to see my father before his time was up because I knew there wasn't much time left. I asked my mom to see my father, and she began to act as if she didn't hear me pleading with her to take me to where he was. They were still trying to pray. Finally, I broke myself from the prayer link and briskly walked into the Intensive Care Unit where my father was laying. When I approached his room, an alarm went off, and doctors started rushing into his hospital room. They were pushing me out of the way, and at that point, I knew my dad had stopped fighting.

After a few minutes, the alarms were turned off and an abrupt silence spread across that hospital floor like a tidal wave. The doctor walked into the waiting room and announced that as of the current time, my father was pronounced dead. Shortly after that moment, my feeling of hurt and pain ran rapid as my heart felt like it had dropped to my feet. A lump entered my throat, forming a blockage not allowing saliva to flow fluently as it did minutes ago. Therefore I couldn't swallow. I began to feel like I couldn't get any air like I did when my friend Smurf committed suicide. My mouth became dry as a desert and my heartbeat sped to the rate of a sports car at its highest speed.

As I finally walked into the room, the lifeless corpse of my father was lying in front of me. I sat there for an hour or so just staring at his body while in my mind begging God to bring him back. I was hoping to see life return to his body, hoping his chest would rise and fall with breath as confirmation. But it didn't happen that way. My father was gone. Edward Garrett Sr. had died, along with my hopes and dreams of finally having a father.

My dad dying was one of the most hurtful times of my life because my dad meant the world to me. I couldn't fathom how someone who had done so little could be loved by someone so much. My mother couldn't understand it as well. I guess beyond loving my father I realized that no matter how good or bad he was…he is still a part of me. So when I lost my father I lost part of myself. I had been in need of his presence in my life for so long, spiritually and emotionally, searching for this father figure, searching for this guy to throw the football with, go fishing with, talk about my first sexual experience with and get fatherly advice. Now I was left to return to that cold, lonely, dark place that I had been to over and over again in my thirteen years of life as a fatherless child.

Unleash the Beast

After my father passed away, I was never the same. Along with the respect of my father's streets course 101: school of hard knocks' beliefs, he convinced me at the time that that any man, young or old, shouldn't cry because it shows weakness; therefore, I didn't cry. I didn't want to be looked at as a weak person. My heart began oozing with pain that overflowed and developed a hardened shell that became cold.

I became a child trapped in the mind and body of a monster. Beginning in middle school when a classmate was trying to be funny and he made a joke about my father. After I asked him what he said, he proceeded to repeat the statement. In a matter of a few seconds, it seemed that I had snapped.

I remember going to punch him, and next thing I remember, I found myself standing over him, punching him in his face, trying my hardest to punch through it. My teacher and a couple of students had to pull me off him. Then, in another class, I was annoyed with a student that I didn't like too much because he always seemed like life wasn't as hard as I knew it could be, judging from my past experiences. He had gotten me in trouble with my teacher and she sent me to the office. Before I walked out, I took my textbook and began to go upside his head with it as if I was trying to beat the knowledge within the text of my thick book into his head on the way out. I thought to myself at the time that I was in trouble anyways, so why wait until after school to beat him up. My thinking became illogical and dangerous. I was very upset and mad, not with him or the guy I beat up previously, but with my father. How could he leave me like this?

How can I be stranded on this earth without the guidance of a father? My dad finally got his act together and promised me a relationship, and now he's gone. My anger toward him was that of a peeved lion after being taunted and poked over and over again until someone opens the cage. I began to feel my life was like a bullet riddled airplane spinning out of control and my attitude was easy to ignite like a live wire. After that, I continued causing trouble in most of my classes and my principal began to know who I was, not for my achievements in school, but for my violent behavior.

My mother could see that I was headed down the wrong path. My friends knew me as Big D, a fighter at school not afraid to face anyone. I was fighting all the time as my life continued on that path of a downward spiral. I began doing things that I never thought Id do, like smoking weed and stealing from people. I cared about nobody but myself. I even lost faith in God. I would ask myself what kind of God would do this to me if he loved me. If God knew all things, he should know that I needed my father around. But as I grew, answers to those questions revealed themselves slowly. I also realized that I had not totally gone insane as well because things had occurred to prove to me that I still had a conscience.

One night, I went into my mother's purse, and she had $200 in it. I was going to take it, but when I grabbed it, in my mind, I flashed back to a time that I recalled her telling me about how my dad stole out of her purse so he could have drug money. I put the money back in her purse because I didn't want to be considered the coward I felt my dad was. Instead of stealing from my mother, I started stealing candy from the local store to sell at school and make some money. Slowly but surely, I made enough money to venture into other products. That candy soon turned into marijuana and later Crack Cocaine. My mother had worked hard and struggled to get me what she could and I noticed, so I didn't want to ask for the same type of clothes my friends had because being a fat guy and being poor didn't quite work out too well. One of my mother's biggest goals was to get us out of that apartment in the neighborhood for which we lived in Long Beach, California. So we moved from Long Beach to a house my mother bought in Carson, California. I thought from that point on, things were going to be great, but they just got worse.

My mother had always wanted to give me and my siblings a house with a yard to play in, yet by the time she worked long enough to buy a house, my siblings were grown and I was too old to play in the yard.

Crews Blues

After moving to Carson, California. About 10-15 miles from Long Beach. I attended Curtis Middle School. I didn't know anyone but made a few friends, like my buddy Big Aaron, who was a cool guy, pretty big in size yet was the coolest person I've ever known. There was my boy, Jimmy; he was the hustler. He sold anything he got his hands on to make money. Then there was my boy Anthony aka Tragedy. He was a cool cat and a ladies' man, yet from my point of view he was loyal to an extent. He kind of reminded me of Manolo from the movie *Scarface*. See in *Scarface*, Manolo was Tony Montana's right-hand man. The key characteristic of Manolo is that he's a pretty boy and seems kind of suspect that he couldn't be trusted and that's how Anthony seemed. He never turned on me or anyone else that I knew, but I felt he could at anytime for the right price or woman. Lastly, there was Therein; he looked like he smoked weed all the time because his eyes were so low, but that's just the way he was. They all were good people to know, and I was glad to hang with them during my time at Curtis Middle School. I must admit that when you are the new guy, people always want to test you. On a side note, there were a lot of crews and cliques at that school, and I wasn't about to be part of any of them.

There were so many followers and people just craving to belong. This one crew called the Tillman

Avenue Hustlers were a bunch of guys from a street with that name. The street wasn't located too far from Curtis Middle School, and as a matter of fact, the days I had to walk home, I walked past that street. For some reason, even though I was the kind of kid that minded his own business, these guys decided they had a problem with me and wanted to jump me. That always made me wonder because no matter where I went, it seemed, through life, I had this dark cloud around me that trouble seemed to find me wherever I was. The funny thing is that I fought back when they jumped me and had a few friends that jumped in on my behalf, well, not a few, just my boy, Big Aaron. But the way he helped me it felt like a few friends jumped in.

After the fight stopped, I looked at Aaron and smiled. At that moment, I realized that there are some people that believe in loyalty and friendship. I was taken to the office and written up for causing a riot. I started hanging with Big Aaron and his crew called CONS, an acronym for Creeping On Niggas Slowly, which was also a play off the root word *Cons* from the Converse shoes. Being a part of that crew, I didn't like the feeling of being a follower or what they would call being a soldier. Therefore, I just decided to start my own clique called CMC, Criminal-Minded Crew. How did I come up with that name, you ask? Well, my mom would always tell me that I thought as a criminal also I liked to listen to the album *Criminal Minded* by my favorite rapper KRS-1 and his crew BDP (*Boogie Down Productions*).

I began to look for people that I could trust and share my idea with to form this crew. I can't recall how we met, but I had a buddy named Terrell, one of the coolest guys you could ever know or meet. Like Anthony, Tarrell was from Compton and a ladies man. Terrell was down for his. Terrell was a good friend. When it came to our crew CMC, I was like the captain, but Terrell was like the navigator or, simply put, the backbone of the crew. There was a racquetball court in the back of the school, and every crew or gang member would go up there and hit up (*tag/graffiti*) their crew or gang on the wall and whoever has a problem with the person or crew that was tagged on the wall, they would cross out the crew or gang as a sign of disrespect. You can imagine CMC was being crossed out every other day.

It seemed like every day, CMC's membership grew more and more. People liked us because honestly, we were simply organized. We hung together and stuck together, and when someone would get bullied, we stuck up for them; that's why they became part of us, for the protection I guess. As our membership and notoriety grew, our safety became more endangered. Other cliques and crews were starting to get upset and decided they wanted to fight us. It also got so bad that a local gang showed up to find out what we were all about and shut us down.

As time went on, I was growing more and more worried about my fate in dealing with the streets, I decided to talk with the local gang in my neighborhood about protection. But they required me to get put on, and I had promised myself and my brother Ed that I would never do that. So I told them, "I'm not with that. I'll figure things out on my own."

Adolescent Antics

My first introduction to change was a man that worked at my middle school by the name of Dean Kinsey. One of the most admirable men a person could ever know, he had the likeness of Martin Luther King Jr., Malcolm X, and Marcus Garvey all rolled into one. As a matter of fact, I'm sure in some past life he was some type of civil rights leader, someone great. The way he carried himself just displayed so much integrity and pride. He wore nothing but suits and had this stern Abraham Lincoln look of seriousness on his face. The beard he had didn't make it any better as he carried himself in a manner that demanded nothing but respect from his peers and students alike.

I continued getting in trouble time and time again, placing me in his office on a regular basis. When I got in trouble, he was right there all the time to talk to me and give me words of wisdom, yet I could see the disappointment in his eyes. Knowing that I was disappointing him made me want to do better because I noticed the pattern of my behavior of being bad, and I hated having to go to his office over and over again.

The disappointment everyone had in me would make you think that it was enough for me to change, but it wasn't. I used to tell my mom that I wish Dean Kinsey was my dad, but I said that about a lot of different men throughout my life because I just wanted that good upbringing or training to become a real man. But after my days of dealing with Dean Kinsey, I continued to struggle. I continued to fail in school, fight, and mess up. I just couldn't get it right! It seemed like I was back in the position of getting in trouble over and over again like I had done before. As I returned to school for ninth grade, I continued on my same path of screwing up.

Previously over the summer, I barely passed the eighth grade and had to go to summer school before I went to the ninth grade. I was looking for ways to make money during that summer, so I did stupid things that could have gotten me hurt really bad, like plotting with my best friend Stephen that I've known since elementary school. We would do things like go into my mother's backyard, collect burned grass from the lawn or lawnmower, put it in marijuana baggies, and sell it in summer school. We called it Bunji. This was supposed to be our version of marijuana. Before school started back, I was finally convinced to get put on and initiated into the local gang in my neighborhood.

I began selling drugs for real again but for this Hispanic guy who lived up the block. *It shouldn't be that hard*, I thought to myself after he gave me my first ounce to sell; besides, I've done this before for my brother when I was just seven and on my own when I was twelve. So it shouldn't be as hard as toting backpacks from place to place like before. Over that summer, I flipped (*selling the entire product*) it so quick that I began to gain a little trust with the man that I sold for. He gave me more and more each time I completely sold the previous batch and gave his money right back to him.

Upon my return to school for my ninth grade year, we added more guys to the crew over the summer. We were now strong. I had the backup, and I wasn't going to be stopped. I had a CMC member's little brother that wanted to be down with us. I didn't let him join though. I told him, "You are too young for this lifestyle," as if I wasn't. He wanted to make some money, so since I started at such a young age, I told him to help me sell weed at school.

This crazy nut decided to really sell it as if it was legal as he ran though the hallways, yelling, "I got weed for sale. Check it out." I shook my head when I saw this, and as I went to go get on his case and ask him what the hell he was doing, a teacher approached him and asked him what he just said, then searched and found three zips (a Ziploc sandwich bag of marijuana) on him. I'm thinking I'm in big trouble because he's definitely going to snitch on me. By now, I'm scared out of my mind of getting caught and going to jail. I realized I have to take the punishment. For some reason, I guess my eye for loyalty was good because he didn't snitch. He got kicked out and sent to juvy (juvenile hall). The thought to come forward and admit the weed was mine all along crossed my mind over and over again as the guilt weighed heavily on my conscience. I remained silent and I never saw him again. After I thought I was off the hook, the rain cloud of trouble had found me again.

I had people after me since I had done bad things over the previous summer. I felt like it all would catch up to me, so I decided to carry a gun. I couldn't find a real gun on the streets so my friend hooked me up with a BB gun that was an exact replica of a Glock 9mm handgun. I knew I never wanted to kill anyone, including myself, so I felt better with the BB gun for some reason. I carried it every day to school for protection. I had a best friend named Billy. He was like my little brother because we grew up together since infancy. We were changing clothes for gym class, I pulled the gun out and put it in my locker. When I placed it in my locker, he said, "Hey, D, let me see that." I was reluctant to give it to him, but I decided what the hell, he's like my brother so it'll be okay.

As I walked into the gym, all I could see was Billy waving the gun around and laughing and taunting around with it. Next thing I know, security was on Billy real quick and he was taken to the office. As he was escorted to the office, I was thinking to myself that he's my best friend, and he will take the rap like the little homie did from the crew. Not one school period had passed before I got a summons to see Dean Kinsey once again. The last time I got in trouble, Dean Kinsey had already warned me that he did not want to see me in his office again.

When I walked into the office, Billy had his head down, and I looked at him. He lifted his head with tears in his eyes and dropped his head again in shame as he knew that he violated the code that we both were raised on to never snitch. I think he was more worried of the recreational beat down he was about to take from his pops that day though. From that point on, I knew this would be the last draw as my time at Curtis Middle School would soon come to an end.

Divine Intervention

Intervention started as Dean Kinsey called my mother and informed her that something needed to be done about my behavior and my life. I believe that was the deciding factor of what my mother had to do. I was not only expelled and kicked out of school, but was also kicked out of my mother's house with nowhere to go. I started to depend on the people from my hood and lived pillow to post, meaning I slept wherever I could. There were a couple of instances when nobody had a place for me to go. From that point, I decided I had two options: to swallow my pride and go home and try to talk my way back into my mother's house by begging my mother to let me come back home, or I could just be prideful and sleep outside. You can say my pride got the best of me as my conscience conveniently reminded me that nobody wanted me, including my mother. So I went to the local park and sat at the bench by the basketball courts. I didn't make a move. The wind got cold as nothing but neighborhood alley cats and rodents crossed my path.

When I sat on the park bench, the temperature seemed to drop and the winds became colder. I was blanketed by a chilly wind that treated my body as a translucent vessel. I began dozing off to sleep but not yet there. I dreamed and envisioned myself in front of millions, rapping and being this big superstar like Snoop Dogg becoming a representative of the city I'm from, Long Beach. I began to realize how quiet and lonely it is at night. Fear began to set in my heart. I heard the voice of my father in the back of my mind, saying, "Darrius, be a man." I then began to reflect on my days as a little kid. I was the center of attention. My mother would smile when she saw me. Then I thought of the pain that I had caused her, coming home drunk and high all the time. I thought of how ashamed she was of me. I thought about the days prior when I was hungry and I had no money, nobody to depend on, and no way to get food.

I realized that I was going to go to Ralphs, the local grocery store, and just grab something to eat and run out. Things didn't quite work that way. I went into the store, looked around, and walked into the cereal aisle, I grabbed a box of Captain Crunch cereal. I opened it, grabbed a handful, and stuffed it in my mouth like pellets being eaten by Pacman. In the midst of stuffing my face and scratching the root of my mouth with each handful of Captain Crunch cereal, this feeling of being watched came over me. This tall man leaned over me, seeming like he appeared out of nowhere, asking, "Sir, what are you doing?" Many excuses flipped through my mind like that of a Rolodex. The only explanation and option that continuously appeared in my mind was to tell the truth.

"Sir, I'm sorry," I said as I began to confess of my intense hunger while promising to pay them back. He advised that I leave that instant. I walked down the aisle to leave, I turned back around to thank him and he was gone, so I just left the store. I didn't want to get stopped again. Being homeless was one of the worst experiences ever as I felt I had nobody and nothing. I used to ask people for money. When doing this, there is this look that one receives when they are panhandling (*asking for money*), that of no worth, a look of someone that doesn't matter to society. Because of this experience, I began to lose the ability to look people in the eye when I spoke to them. I felt they were better than me. When asking for change, people look at you as if you don't exist and they are looking through you. I realized that I didn't want to live like that; I can't believe another human being can make me feel so transparent. I wanted better in my life. So I swallowed my pride, and I went to my mother's house and began to bang on her door.

My clothes were dirty and dingy from having the same things on for weeks, and the smell of weed and alcohol reeked from my pores as my mother answered the door. "Mom," I said as she slowly cracked her door open. "What, Darrius?"

"Mom, I want to come home," I said. "Darrius, you can't come here. Call your sister," she said as she slammed the door in my face.

I then broke into drastic tears and emotion. "Mom, I don't want to be on the streets no more...please let me in," but she would not let me in. There was no reply. "Mom," I yelled. "I need you." There still was no reply. I sat on the front porch and placed my head in my hands. The door then made a screech noise as it cracked open. Her voice then saying, "Come back tomorrow and I will call your sister. Maybe she will let you live with her, but you cannot live here, Darrius." I then asked,

"Where am I going to go, Mama?" She then got quiet and the door closed again. From that point, I realized something about life. *Sometimes, you have to figure things out on your own.*

I left the house and went back to the park. The cold started to set in, it seemed like it was going to rain. I didn't do too well sleeping on the park bench like I did the night before, so I tried something else. I couldn't find a place to sleep, but I saw this tree that was pretty much like a shrub and climbed into it and laid there. I hummed this song I remember my father singing every time I saw him by Diana Ross that goes, "Reach out and touch somebody's hand. Make this world a better place, a better place if you can." With the wind blowing and nothing but nature around, I kept humming that song, hopeful that tomorrow would be better than today, while I began thinking also of my short fourteen years of life. A tear escaped my left eye, and I gradually drifted off to sleep.

The Toughest Love

The next day, I finally went to my mother's, and she allowed me to take a shower and clean myself up. She said she spoke with my sister and her husband and they were okay with me coming to live with them while I go to school so that I could have a new start. I knew my mother was frustrated, but it hurt me worse to feel that my own mother, the woman that birthed me and gave me life, didn't want me anymore. I left my friends, my crew and my gang behind as well as the drug dealing, or so I thought.

To me, being sent to live with my sister was no better than being sent to a foster home. I loved living with my sister and brother-in-law, but the fact of feeling neglected made me feel like I was in the foster system. Riding in the back of the car a poem came to me that I wrote called:

Far Away

I feel far away
with nowhere to go
Nobody to call mommy, no greatness to show
My inner child lost, to my anger and pain
My feeling of sunshine; filled with clouds and rain
Sometimes I want to die, so I tickles death ears
I'm 2 much of a coward when death is near
I'm but only a human, trying to figure the way

So sad that my mother let me go astray
Tell my mother I'll figure it out
but not today, Cause I'm still hurt inside
Cause we're so far away

Coming out of my poetic trance, I began to realize, *No graduation from the ninth grade for me, I guess.* Long Beach School District high schools started at the ninth grade level. Therefore, since my old school district middle schools went up to the ninth grade, I never received a formal graduation from middle school to high school. But my journey continued to a place I never thought I'd be, Woodrow Wilson High School aka Pleasantville.

Hello, Pleasantville

5:00 am, I'm a bit tired. The darkness that covered the city started to unveil as the sun slowly rose. As I woke up, I slowly wiped the sleep out of my eyes. I was kind of excited because I'm going to an actual high school. I didn't get to graduate from middle school like the other students. I felt a bit bad yet privileged to be with the older group in high school. I must admit it felt like I was just dumped into high school and didn't get to experience orientation or an introduction to high school life. I guess you can say that I'm going to receive a crash course. Stepping off the school bus, seeing all of these preppy white kids, kind of scared me because I didn't know what to expect and people are usually fearful of the unknown. As my bus pulled up, I could remember thinking to myself that I may not make it past a day without getting in some kind of trouble.

I got off the bus, and a couple of white kids looked at me as if they were saying "He wouldn't make it past a day," just as I had thought. Entering the front of the school, I was mesmerized by the classic higher learning type of look to it, kind of like an old college. As I started to walk inside, I was greeted by an old lady that seemed like she was in a rush, asking me my last name. "Garrett," I replied. Then she looked down this long list. "G…G…Ga…Gar…Garcia…Garrard… oh, Garrett, your homeroom is room 213 in the 200 building to your left." I grabbed my bag and went into the classroom. Nothing but Mexicans, but I had no problem with that knowing all my time in junior high my name was close to Garcia, Gonzales, and Gomez , so I was okay with it.

But with the inner city beef between blacks and Mexicans, I was unsure if being in my homeroom would be considered as a good idea or a death wish! But I'm not worried. There's nothing that can happen here that didn't happen in my neighborhood. So I should be fine. The teacher walks in the classroom and started to pass out our schedules, and I'm still trying to figure out how I am supposed to make it in this school. As the schedule falls on my desk, I look at it and see Math, English, Reading...wait, Reading? I can read. What the hell they got me in a reading class for? PE? I can't believe they have me taking PE again. As time passed, I learned to accept it and moved on. From that first day of school for me, I realized it was going to take some time to get used to this. As I walked through the school, it seemed so big. I just can't wait to get this day over with or at least get to the period I like most, lunch.

As I sat in my class, lunch time was approaching, and I was overjoyed because my stomach was singing old Negro spirituals since I had failed to eat before I came to school. When the bell rang, I got up and walked outside, and sure enough, it was packed from one side to the other. It almost looked like a prison yard. I glanced across the way, I saw all the Asians in one area, the Mexicans in another, and the athletes by the stairs of the 100 building. My thoughts were not focused on who I would hang out with or who would accept me, but where could I get a slice of pizza and a Pepsi from. I continued on the same path until I started realizing that there was a difference between myself and the students at my school.

The other students were all dressed up and I was not. I realized at that moment I had to do something and I had to do it quick. I went through this dilemma in middle school, and I refused to go through it again, not having the same clothes that my friends had. My mind went back to when I had the most money in my life and that was when I sold drugs. Moving back to Long Beach, being expelled from school, and being kicked out of my mother's house made me realize I was going to have a new start in Long Beach and I wanted to release this curse of bad luck and trouble that followed me everywhere I went.

As time went on, I began to make a few friends and became more involved in playing football, yet I continued to dabble in the ways of my past by selling weed on the side. I didn't think too much of it because I was very casual in selling it. I didn't flash it around or let anyone know I sold drugs unless I knew without a shadow of a doubt that they smoked it. Time passed as I continued on and found myself in a class where the teacher was not too fascinated with her students. She just sat there at times and advised us to do some crazy word problems while she just did nothing but sat at her desk and walked around sort of like a babysitter. So of course, I let her babysit me. I sat there and looked at her like she was crazy and didn't do much work at all while she read her paper. After some time passed, this lady walked in with this pep in her step. She seemed very happy, yet I was trying to figure out why. Whatever she was smoking, I wanted some of that. I know people would swamp me trying to get a hold of that kind of drug. If I was the street pharmacist guru, I'd say that it seemed as if she was mixing weed with Vicodin.

All I know she was happy with life or at least seemed like it, and to me, that was considered as crazy. She seemed sincere about teaching and didn't seem racist like a lot of teachers I've encountered here. When she walked out of the classroom, my teacher then gave her a mean look when she left like this woman was crazy. I continued seeing this teacher around campus most of the year until I encountered a situation that changed the rest of my life.

Dare, Drugs, and Thugs

I was at school with drugs on me. Now, I usually didn't keep it on me for a long time. I was stuck in a situation where someone asked for me to bring them quite a large quantity, and I decided what the hell. I need the money anyway. I brought it to school, and the person didn't show up that day. I got word that they were doing a check for drugs in lockers by bringing a drug-sniffing K9 through the school and have the dogs sniff the lockers. So I kept it on me. I was on the way from the location where I was supposed to meet my buyer, trying to get to my next period class, but the bell rang. I darted off to try and catch my class before the door closed. I was caught by the same lady that showed me my homeroom when I first came to the school. "Young man," she said. I looked her way, then kept walking. "Young man, come here," she shouted. I began walking faster. She caught up to me, then advised that I should go to OCS (*an acronym for On Campus Suspension*) that instant.

I don't remember what I said to her, but I kind of mumbled some crazy comment and commenced to walk across campus to OCS. I stood in line, waiting for my turn to be checked in. When I stepped up to the desk, the frail, dreadlocked man responded in a small, quiet voice to see my ID. I reached in my back pocket, pulled out my wallet, and a nickel bag of weed fell to the ground. Thinking that he didn't see it, I quickly placed my foot on it. He then looked at me with a look of "I know this guy isn't that stupid to bring drugs to school." He looked below the table. He advised me to move my foot, I began to ask, "Why?" That was a big mistake. It made me look even guiltier. He then asked me to follow him. He picked up the baggy of weed and sat me in the back room.

The police arrived, and the face of the guy that arrested me seemed familiar. I was searched, and they asked if I had anything else on me. I responded, "No," then the officer grabbed my bag and asked if I had any weapons before they search me or my stuff. I was sweating and my heart was beating rapidly. He started to unzip my bag, and I grew more and more nervous with each zip that he undid on my backpack. By time he totally opened my backpack, I shouted, "It's more in there." He looked at me, and they looked into the backpack.

He reached into the backpack, pulling out what was luckily a little bit short of an ounce of marijuana. Had it been more than an ounce, I would have been prosecuted with possession and sales. Although they still tried to slap me with the intent to sell, somehow they were able to downgrade it to a misdemeanor later on. I was escorted through the school and out the front of the school as school let out for the day. Students were all over the place. The friends I made were walking up to me, asking me what I did and what am I going to jail for? At first, I must admit, I felt like a real bad ass, but as I walked out in handcuffs and people were pointing and laughing, I felt like more of a dumb ass.

They placed me in the car and drove around the school. Honestly, it felt like they knew students were laughing, so they took me on a victory lap around the school as they circled twice. The cold backseat of that squad car was something that I never ever wanted to experience again in life. I've been in a squad car once before when my friend shot himself, but I didn't feel the feeling I felt knowing I was on my way to jail. As I got out the car, they then brought me in, and I realized that there was no turning back from where I am now. I was told to sit down until my name was called. At that time, it hit me as I realized that my life was about nothing and had no purpose. I was called up by the officer doing paperwork, and he asked me my name. I responded, "Darrius, sir." He sat back, looked at me, and shook his head. "Didn't you go to a school called Minnie Gant Elementary?"

"Yes," I said.

"You don't remember me, do you?"

"No, but you do look familiar," I said. He then proceeded to remind me that he was my DARE officer when I was in the fifth grade.

DARE stands for Drug Abuse Resistance and Education. It is a drug abuse prevention education program designed to equip elementary and middle school children with knowledge about drug abuse, the consequences of abuse, and skills for resisting peer pressure to experiment with drugs, alcohol, and tobacco.

I felt so guilty finding out who this officer was; but I was more disgusted with who I had become— the person that the government and school districts spent hundreds of dollars for police officers to teach me not to be. Yet this was who I am. A drug dealer.

Something Better

I knew from that moment on that things would not be the same. I took it all as a sign, the way things happened to me as a message that I needed to change. From bringing the large amount of weed that I usually don't bring to school, to the K9 dog coming to the school, to my buyer not showing up, to being arrested by my DARE officer. Funny thing is I was really good in that DARE class as I already knew about half the drugs we talked about by the age of thirteen. I realized that all of this meant something for me. I needed to listen because there was something better for me, and I was going to find it— or maybe it would find me.

Being in jail gives me the creeps. And who gets arrested by their DARE officer? As the cuffs were coming off, all I could do was hear the voice of my DARE officer in the back of my head from back when I was in his class, saying, "Don't do or sell drugs because I don't want to have to be the one to arrest you." I never thought or dreamed that four to five years later I would be the one he was speaking of as the person who could get caught. I was too good. Now it's inevitable that I am going to wind up like my brother and father, in and out of jail. I know I am about to do some major time. Long Beach PD does not play when going on trial for possession and sales of narcotics, although I knew that wouldn't be my charge. I was sure the intent to sell wouldn't be any better.

After the officer called me up and revealed who he was, he asked me a bunch of questions. Name, age, stuff like that. But one question I will never forget as he was booking me was, "Are you a gang member?" I replied, "Uh, nah...no. I don't do that." He then leaned forward and said, "Look, kid, it makes me no mind, this is for your protection." A thick lump invaded my throat as I swallowed and said, "Yea...uh. Yeah, I am." After I did that, all I saw was this big red stamp he put on my file that said *gang member* in all red capital letters.

All I could think of is how I once again became a disappointment to my mother and the rest of my family. I was already giving my sister and brother-in-law problems. I knew this was the last draw for them. *Homeless again, I guess*, I silently whispered to myself then rested my head back on the wall, trying to decipher my life's path, thinking of all the heartache and pain I have caused my mother and all the people I have lost to the foolishness going on in the streets. I thought about how far I could really get selling drugs and realized it can't be too far. I saw too many people build an empire from slanging and lose it all, including the things they bought with legal money as well was ceased also when the drug dealers were arrested in my neighborhood.

While sitting on that cold, hard wooden bench, time had passed and I grew very tired. I drifted off to sleep as I begin to have this vision again of me in front of this crowd of millions cheering me on and clapping their hands. I guess daydreaming became part of my life now. As I was saying my tightest rhyme, people were screaming my name, but they were calling me by my last name only for some reason: "Garrett! Garrett! Garrett! Garrett!" As I started to hug the cute girl in the front row, they began cheering harder and harder. "Garrett! Garrett! Garrett! Garrett!" the crowds' voices then united to one deep, manly voice. I was awakened to my name being yelled by a heavyset drill sergeant–looking police officer. "Garrett! You're being bailed out." I was happy that I was leaving. Also I was a bit afraid to be leaving as well because I knew that I was going to have to face my mother's disappointment once again.

After I was released, I was greeted by my mother, sister, and brother-in-law. I don't recall what was said, yet I knew that I wound up not living with my sister anymore. I lived with my mother again, and it was interesting. I met with the assistant principal at Wilson High and he was a great guy because usually they don't allow people back into the district after doing what I had done. The principal allowed me to come back on the basis that I concentrated on my studies, continued to try and excel in football, go to rehab for drug use, and be part of this new program called LINKS.

That didn't seem like that big of a deal. I can do that. The best was yet to come. I began my new classes and went into this classroom with students that seemed like they all had issues. Like I didn't have problems of my own. I sat in the back of the class so I could watch everyone else. When the bell rang, this lady is in the class and is writing on the board in cursive. She seems familiar, and the voice sounds familiar as well. As she's writing, I began to think to myself, *Wait, I know this lady.* The clothes also look familiar when she turned around I then remembered. "Wait, that crazy lady that's happy all the time." She took her hand and pushed her hair behind her ear and said the words that began the first day of my journey to a better life. "Good morning, class. My name is Ms. Gruwell."

Back to Pleasantville

Being in this class was no different from any other class or so I thought. I felt the stares of people different from me piercing my soul. Some with hatred, some with questions. I'm sure they're possibly wondering what gang am I from. Or how long I can last in this class? No matter what, I was there for a purpose, and I was not about to let nobody stop me for any reason. My purpose was to finally try to do something with my life. But it's hard to do that when everyone already looks at me as a gang member, threat, or maybe a failure. My dad was a failure, and I had no reason to think that I was any better than him since that's the person my mother saw when she looked at me.

I know that sometimes when she looked at me and get mad that it's not me, it's my father that she saw because I looked so much like him. I never knew that a man could hurt a woman so badly. I didn't get much encouragement from her because she was the type of person that felt putting someone down would bring them up. Like reverse psychology. If someone tells me that I can't do something, it influences me to think the opposite just to prove them wrong. But when it came to my mother, whatever she told me, I believed it. So if she said I'm not going to be anything in life, I believed her. But who is she to tell me what I can't do or become right? I could be a president or a lawyer if I wanted.

Yeah, right. I could see it now. President Darrius Garrett, the smooth-talking ex–gang member with two counts of drug possession on his record. Now that I think about it: smooth talker, run-ins with the law, drug possession, maybe I would have a pretty good chance with politics. But through it all, I realized that something needed to change in my life. The dreams of being a star and being a somebody worth something in the world continued to paint pictures beyond the canvas of my mind of what life could be for me. If I could just be successful, I know my mom would love me more. If I could do something spectacular, I know I would finally be accepted among my peers.

Sitting in this English class, I realize that I am in the class of the lady that seem like she is just so happy all the time. As happy as she is, I know she has to be smoking that bomb Kush (*type of marijuana*). As for me, I will just sit here and watch everything and everybody because I already know that most of them already are looking for me to start trouble, but they have another thing coming. This time, I want to make my mom proud, yet I always wind up in trouble.

Something in me has to change. I just don't know when or how. But here in Wilson High aka "Pleasantville" is where I'm confident my change will take place.

My Investigation Report

Time had passed, and I began to find out more and more about the people around me including my teacher, Ms. Gruwell, a young college grad with the luxuries of life handed to her, or so I thought. You would have thought she didn't have a care in the world. My perception of her was that she may not be crazy, but it was weird to me that she walked around happy with life. What was it about her life that made her so freaking happy? I admit her personality was infectious. At times, it seemed that I was happy through her happiness. I began to feed off her energy each day, and I looked forward to going to her classroom more and more. The more I was around her, the more I wanted to learn about her. I didn't realize that she was so young though. Being a teacher at the age twenty-three obviously meant she must have been interested in educating us because she could have been anything else in the world other than a teacher.

I didn't think that at her age I would have ever been able to babysit bad-ass students. I would have ended up in jail immediately. I saw teachers get beat up all the time, and I knew if I was this Gruwell lady, I would have come to school with a gun, hunting knife, and two Rottweiler dogs guarding both sides of my desk. She seemed so vulnerable and trusting of everyone. I hope someone tells her to tuck those pearls before someone snatches them. I had to admit that it felt good for someone to trust me for a change. Usually, the white women in the area would clutch their purses, look away, or cross the street altogether just to avoid any interaction or possibilities of me saying hello. What? Gangsters, thugs, and drug dealers couldn't have manners?

Later that day, football practice had just ended as I walked into the locker room, and I had a feeling that something was wrong. As I entered, from a slight distance, I could see the door of my locker slightly opened as if I had forgotten to close it. The old lock that I put on there was broken, revealing that my locker had been broken into. Glancing into my locker, I saw that my wallet and my watch were gone, along with the ring that my mother had bought for me last Christmas. A gust of anger and rage filled my mind so I slammed my locker door as hard as I could and punched a dent into it with all my might. Walking out of the locker room, thoughts of how my mother wouldn't believe that someone had stolen my ring crossed my mind. She would definitely think I sold it for money.

While I stood outside the football locker room, I began to think beyond the ring and wondered how the hell I was going to get home since I had to take the bus over twenty miles to get there. Within the distance, I saw a green mini SUV driving through the campus. It was my teacher, Ms. Gruwell. She asked if I was okay, and I began to cry. I explained how my things had been stolen and I didn't have a way home. She then said, "Oh, I can take you home."

Although I would have appreciated the ride, it would have been quite embarrassing if she took me home and saw the guys that I hung out with from the gang. I thought she might begin to judge me based off that. I told her, "No, that's okay." However, she insisted over and over again until I gave in. Those thoughts of her judging me opposed to the fact that I lived too far from my school played angel and devil on my shoulder as I timidly decided to hop into the green mini SUV. As she drove away and took me home. From that point on, I realized that she was someone that I could really count on. At that moment, I realized that she had won the first installment of my trust. *This woman really cares*, I said to myself. Erin Gruwell, along with my middle school dean, Dean Kinsey, helped create the first cracks in the outer shell of my hardened heart to unleash the love, loyalty, and warmth trapped inside.

Books, Books, Books

Walking into room 203, I noticed that new books were placed around the room, such as *The Color Purple* by Alice Walker, *Night* by Elie Wiesel, *Jesse* by Gary Soto, *The Wave* by Todd Strasser, *Zlata's Diary: A Child's Life in Sarajevo* by Zlata Filapovic, *Animal Farm* by George Orwell, and this book with a black-and-white photo on it of a young girl named Anne Frank. When I saw this, I realized that none of these books had anything to do with me and had no interest. I didn't see a black dude in front of any of these books, but I felt maybe I could get into *The Color Purple* since I loved the movie. It was pretty dope, so I thought the book should be even better. Although the story line was good, I couldn't get into *The Color Purple*. I read *Night* and it was interesting, yet I still was unable to understand or grasp what I was reading.

I really enjoyed *The Wave* because it talked about this classroom that was actually, I would say, brainwashed. Although it started out as a class project, it showed how a group of people could honestly be controlled. Then reading *Animal Farm* made me really think about how people are, and about for the next month or so, I was either comparing people to Napoleon, Boxer, or Molly. I truly appreciated how Mr. Orwell was able to talk about modern times and political issues subliminally through this story. That exercised my first thoughts of becoming an author myself because I like telling stories but to be able to give my honest feelings about things subliminally through telling a regular story interested me, as I knew I had a lot to say. However, no other book captivated me as much as *The Diary of Anne Frank.*

It was a warm day when I went to the neighborhood library. I walked up and down the aisles, looking for this book because we had left our books at school.

The one thing that really stuck with me when reading was the part about Anne having admitted to feeling like a bird with its wings clipped because of how she had been stuck in the attic. I was really able to empathize with her. I recalled being locked in our two-bedroom apartment. My mother would make me stay inside, trying to protect me from all of the violence that was going on outside. Still, I was able to watch things unfold since the only view the window to our apartment had was to the alley. In that alley, a lot of things went on from rapes and murders to arrest and cop chases.

I decided to read on more and more with envy as she talked about her relationship with her father Otto Frank bringing forth reminiscent times of my father and I. To me, this all became nothing but a modern soap opera. I got so into the book that time seemed to fly by to the point where they advised everyone that the library would be closing in the next fifteen minutes. I was so into what I was reading that I did not want to put the book down. I was too engulfed in what was occurring. I began reading faster but I was already to the point where I couldn't even comprehend what I was reading anymore. "Ten minutes till closing," the librarian said. I continued trying to read but wasn't getting anywhere. "Five minutes till closing," she said. I looked around and began to walk back to the bookshelf where I originally got the book.

The book was too interesting for me to put back and I didn't want anyone to come and pick it up. I felt good about being able to read beyond where I felt others were reading in my class. Maybe I could even show up to class and know everything about the book. So I decided to do what any interested reader would do. I stole the book.

Hello, Jones,
Nice to Meet You

Being in the links program allowed me to meet a lot of people that I probably would not have taken the time to get to know or that probably would not have taken the time to know me. It was funny that we all had differences, yet we were also similar at the same time. We all came from different backgrounds, like my buddy Jay. He was a cool dude, very light in skin tone as if he was mixed with black and white. His parents worked at the school. So I'm sure it was important that he remained on his best behavior. I envied how Jay was able to go to lunch earlier than everyone else did, especially since lunch was my favorite period of the day. At that time, I didn't know that he was a diabetic though. Then there was the girl that was from my point of view the prettiest girl in school; her name was Mella. I had never seen anyone so beautiful except for on television.

What made her even more beautiful was the fact that she had a nice personality. She wasn't afraid to talk to or befriend anyone. Usually, girls that knew they were pretty came along with ugly personalities but not her. Then there was Jones. Now, Jones didn't play or at least he looked like he didn't. When you looked at Jones, it seemed like he had a lot of pain and hurt. I would never forget how he and I met officially.

See, I had met this girl by the name of Metrie. Honestly, Metrie was not someone who people that knew me would consider as my type, yet Metrie had something about her that interested me. I personally think it was her sex appeal; she was more developed for her age, putting other girls' bodies to shame. Or maybe it was just the fact that she seemed very dark and to herself that really appealed to me. As time progressed, we began to hang out with each other a little more. The more we spent time, the more I began to like her. There was another side that Metrie possessed, but I never understood. When she came to school, I would see scratches and bruises on her arms. It looked like she had made attempts to hurt, or even kill, herself.

When I tried to talk to her about it, she would get very defensive and advise me not to talk about it so I would just let it go. Another subject that I would bring up was her past boyfriends. That was when I found out that she had shared a pretty interesting relationship with the likeness of Jones. She would share stories with me about how Jones had done her wrong and how mean he was. She built Jones up to look like a complete asshole. When I had the opportunity to meet Jones, we were both on the track team; I did field events and he ran track. I began to develop a strong dislike for Jones because I couldn't understand how a guy could treat someone so badly.

A rumor was started that he wanted to fight me and I wanted to fight him. When I would see Jones around campus or on the field, I would give him a cold look, mad dogging him, thinking to myself that I could care less about who he was, giving him the sign that we could always square off if he really wanted to fight me. I guess you could say we called each other's bluff because it was supposed to go down after school. We were supposed to meet up and fight till the death or till one of us got tired, whichever happened first. While in my last class, I glanced at the clock and it seemed that 2:45 p.m. had come in no time when the final bell rang. I grabbed my backpack and went to meet my fate. My heart was beating fast with my adrenaline pumping and my hands sweating. I asked myself, *Are you really scared of this punk?* Whether I was or wasn't, I was not going to let this dude take my woman or my pride.

As we met up, I guess he was having the same thoughts as he actually showed up, so I have to do what I have to do then. But before we could even get into it, something definitely out of the ordinary happen. Jones said that he didn't want to fight. As much as I didn't either, I was more relieved than anything to hear that, yet we had to get to the bottom of the problem. The more we talked, the better we were able to work out our differences. He and I both realized that Metrie was playing us both. She was telling Jones about me and telling me about Jones.

We both decided and agreed to leave her alone. I guess you could say I made the first move when I told her I was done. It was odd that she hadn't asked any questions. I didn't hear anything about Jones making his move though. Days later, when I was walking out of my class for lunch I glanced across campus and saw her walking with this other guy. His arm was around her neck, and they were walking and laughing. I shook my head in disbelief as the guy turned his head. To my surprise, it was a familiar face that I recognized. It was Jones.

Wanting to Change for a Change

Now that we have read the books, did various projects, and wrote book reports on the authors, Ms. Gruwell decided to bring all of her classes together. I was so used to the people already in my class I could care less about the people that were from the other classes. As we moved our desk around, other students flocked in. But as I sat and watched the other students walked in, one who I considered an arch nemesis entered the room, Jones. What the hell is he doing in my class? I couldn't believe it. I looked at him with a deceitful stare as he sat across the room. My mind went back to how he basically took my girl from right under me while making me think we were both going to leave her alone. Yet the class began discussing the books we read, and my dislike for Jones was stored away for a later time. We realized that we wanted something more, just as the authors that wrote the books we were reading wanted. We wanted change.

See, when you think about it, that's why the authors were telling the stories: for change. Like *The Joy Luck Club* was about change. *The Color Purple* was about change as well. It may not be about change from good to bad but maybe from bad to good or maybe from one status to the other, yet at the end, the result to the reader brings change. Be it change of heart, change of thinking, or even change of behavior. A lot of us students wanted change but didn't know how to change or where to start. I for one was guilty of that. I decided that I wanted to change a long time ago. I would honestly say besides my encounters from the drive-by when I was young to my situation in junior high school being influenced by Dean Kinsey. I also had another encounter that really made me realize that the street life was not for me.

It was a hot, sunny southern California day in 1995 as I was out on the corner of my block, hanging out with my buddies doing what I did naturally: slangin' (*selling drugs*). A woman came up to me and she asked me for a nickel rock (*$5 worth of drugs*). I advised her that I would be more than willing to take care of that. She then advised me that she didn't have any money yet, but she can offer me various things for collateral until she gets her money on the first. I thought about it for a minute and realize the things that she had to offer I already had: a television, radio, Walkman, Discman, etc., therefore I told her, "There's nothing that you can give me that I don't have already." The woman then looked to the left, then to the right to make sure my buddies weren't paying attention and leaned forward and whispered, "I will let you hit this if you give me credit, and I will still pay you back when I get the money on the first." Once I declined her offer, she then walked off, and in the midst of her storming off, she then stopped and turned back around.

She walked back to where I was and looked at me for a minute and asked me how old I was. I told her,

"You don't need to know how old I am." She then asked me was I an adult and I said no. She stepped back for a minute as a slight grin approaches her face. She then says, "I have a daughter: she should be around your age, maybe a lot younger. If you hook me up, I'll let you have your way with her, she does what I say so you shouldn't have no problems." After hearing her say that, I got really upset. I believe that was the first time that I sincerely thought about hitting a woman. Instead, I grabbed both of her shoulders and pushed her away from me telling her to "get away quick before I did something that I'll regret." As she walked away, all I could think about from that day forward was that little girl and what was to ever become of her if her mother approached someone else with that same offer that would take her up on it and steal the young girl's innocence.

From that day forward, I never saw her again. It became more and more common as I got older and was exposed to more things on the streets. I began to become numb to violence. Numb to abuse, and with the loss of dozens of friends, I became numb to death. By this time I had seen people die and I didn't want to see anymore. I began to think to myself that I am meant for better because I had a kind heart and I cared about people. But one of my first lessons in change was the only way to have better is to simply do better.

Rabbi's and Prime Rib

I heard Ms. Gruwell had taken her students before to a movie called *Schindler's List*, and they were heavily discriminated against. Now we're going to the Museum of Tolerance and this restaurant called Lawry's in Beverly Hills, California. I don't care if we were going down the street and turning back around, it just felt good to go on a field trip. I didn't think about the reason why she was taking us to this place, but I guess we all would soon find out.

As we were on the bus, we began talking. I heard someone beat boxing in the back of the bus; that was my cue. Anytime I hear beat boxing, I had to freestyle. It was just in my blood. As I began to say my rhymes, the group was really digging it. Then here comes Jones with his lyrics. Although I should be over the whole Metrie situation, I decided to try and come with a better freestyle to outshine his. Before I knew it, we were going back and forth. Between Jones and I, it was a battle. To the other students, it was a wonderful form of entertainment while we were on our way to the museum. We freestyled until the bus stopped at the Museum of Tolerance and continued until we got in the building.

Inside the Simon Wiesenthal Museum of Tolerance, we entered into this room. We got the opportunity to watch the movie *Schindler's List* like Ms. Gruwell's previous students. I was so amazed by this movie; I thought it would be the sorriest movie ever. The movie was so raw to how things were during the Holocaust. I was very into it. I tried to trick myself by saying that "its just a movie and not real" to keep from crying. I began to empathize with the children that were portrayed in the movie as I know how it feels to be so young and watch people die around me.

After seeing the movie, we were taken on a tour. This was a tour like no other as we were given these cards like passports and they had a child on them. As we went through the tour, it showed things such as simulated death camps and the propaganda that was sent around to make people believe that Jews were like rats. When I saw that, I thought about what my dad taught me about what a rat is and I wondered is that because Jews snitched on people? But I quickly realized that it was because of what Adolf Hitler trained the people to believe.

As we went through the exhibit, we saw the genocide that occurred in the death camps and heard stories from survivors of what happened during the times that they were in hiding. I can't imagine how that would feel to have my family torn apart. I couldn't imagine being taken away from my mother against both of our wills. As we got to the end of the exhibit, I entered my pass and found out that the little girl that was on my pass died. She didn't make it out of the camp. That was so sad that so many people lost their lives for nothing. Just because someone didn't like them and taught others not to like them as well. As we left the museum, I realized one thing about the holocaust: it was real, very real.

After leaving, it was very quiet on the bus. Some people were crying, some were at a lost for words, and others such as myself were just thinking. I thought to myself, *why didn't somebody do anything?* The only answer I could think of was the answer that my father would have given me: it's not my business. I'm sure that's what the US and other countries thought at that time. They felt it wasn't their business. But I then thought to myself, *What if someone was trying to kill me and my family?* Would it be okay for someone to walk by and not help me, simply because it's not their business?

As I was deep in thought, the bus stopped, and they asked for everyone to get off the bus. We arrived at this restaurant called Lawry's Prime Rib. This has got to be the best restaurant ever; I have never been to a place like this. I was amazed at the way they served the food and the way that it tasted. The presentation of the food was amazing to me because they brought it to our tables and served it onto our plates. Then a chef came and served the vegetables and another guy brought the prime rib to the table, sliced it for us, and served it. I had never eaten something so wonderful in my life. The vegetables were so good, buttery and edible. The mashed potatoes were like clouds in my mouth so light and fluffy, the prime rib was the tenderest slice of prime rib I have ever had. Since the streets were all that I knew, my only comparison to this dish was that of a last meal before execution. We all ate so much that we filled our little bellies beyond being full.

Now I know why college football teams come here before bowl games and big celebrations because this is definitely a championship meal. That of which if I died afterward, I would have died with a full stomach and happy. We all had become sick from eating so much. But understand that when you haven't had anything like that before; you tend to try and get all you can because you know you may never have that experience ever again in life. I'm sure that was the logic behind most of our indulgence and overeating that day. On our way out, I thought to myself how expensive this place was. While I was stepping onto the bus, I stopped, looked back, and said the great quote of the Terminator: "I'll be back."

A Friendship
Defined by a Line

A screech from the masking tape being put on the floor awoke me from my daydream of my previous encounters that influenced me to want change in my life. Ms. Gruwell made one line straight down the room with the tape. She explained the rules of the line game. She prepared us that this game is important; so answer truthfully. So we commenced to playing. She then asked, "Who heard the latest Snoop Doggy Dogg album, *Step out on the Line*?" Everyone stepped out there. Then the questions got a bit harder when she asked, "How many people ate lunch today?" Still, it was almost everyone out there accept for me and a few others. She then followed that with other questions. Then as she noticed we were getting used to sharing our stories by standing on the line, she got harder with her questions. She then asked, "How many people are in gangs?" No one stepped to the line. At that time, she's figured out that we weren't stupid enough to incriminate ourselves. She then twisted the words a little and asked the correct question to get the right answer by rephrasing the question, saying, "How many people know someone that is in a gang?" Half the class stepped to the line, including myself.

Her next round of questions were questions that I personally feel defined and began a lifelong friendship.

"How many of you have been shot at?" Again, half the classroom stepped to the middle. "Okay" she said, "how many people have actually been shot?" Only a few remained in the middle. "How many people have lost a friend to gang violence or drugs?" Over half of the class stepped to the middle of the classroom. "How many have lost five?" Most people stayed there. "How many people lost fifteen?" Half of that group then left, yet there were two people left standing on that line. It was me staring at the ground with shame, feeling very embarrassed and singled out. I lifted my head a bit from shame only to see one standing on the line along with me at the other side of the room. It was Jones.

A bond had now been subliminally created. She continued to move up the numbers until even Jones stepped away from the line. And once again, just as I felt when my father had left me stranded on that porch when I was younger, I stood there alone as I had lost over thirty-five people, including friends and family members to gangs, violence and drugs. Who would ever know that people went through the same things that I did, although I'm still upset that Jones lied and took my girl. Maybe now, I have met someone that finally knows where I am coming from.

Ms. Gruwell came up with an idea as she then said, "I have an assignment for you guys. Lately, you all have been reading the books, and one of the latest books that you guys have read is *Zlatas Diary*, and unlike Anne Frank, Zlata is still living. As you see, she was involved, just as Anne Frank, in a war that tore her country apart.

Although it would not be considered as a civil war or any other war that could have occurred within our nation, you all yourselves are involved in an undeclared war with the gang violence and deaths. So my assignment to you is to write Zlata letters to let her know how you feel." Then a student said, "Hey, why don't we invite her to Long Beach?" We began to write our letters and history was made as we received a response that Zlata would be joining us in Newport Beach, California.

Meeting Zlata was a dream come true; the reason why I say that is because I, as well as some of the other students in my class, have never met a real author before. There was pure pandemonium. It seemed as everyone was there from Jones to my friend Chad, Jay, and another friend of mine, who was from the neighborhood I was from, named Laz. We were all very glad to have her in our presence. But we were also even more excited to be outside of Long Beach. The place that we had dinner at was so beautiful. We also brought our parents. We laughed, took photos, and had an all-out good time with her. This was one of the first events that we had where I was able to bring my mother, and she was not worried about receiving a bad report about who I was as a person or as a student. As my mother and I were on our way home, she then asked me to tell her a little more about who Zlata was, so I explained to her, yet I began to speak more about Anne Frank.

My mother seemed very intrigued at the fact that I was so inspired by someone that wasn't a rapper, football player, or gangster. Yet I was more intrigued by the fact that I read a whole book from cover to cover. It seemed that my mother had began to gain a little more trust in me once again and believe that I can do something that my father nor my brother had done: graduate from high school.

Miep and Me

We came back from our weekend, and we were very happy about meeting with Zlata. We were very happy and fulfilled with the things that we had accomplished by bringing someone from across the world just to meet with us. By this time, we were all on a high that no one can explain because it was the feeling that we can do anything. So be it that we brought Zlata to our town. We decided since Anne Frank is not alive, let's bring someone from her time such as a Holocaust survivor to our class next. From that point, we met a woman by the name of Gerda Cipher, as well as another Holocaust survivor by the name of Renée Firestone.

It's very interesting that we got the opportunity to meet Renée because the fact that she had worked with Steven Spielberg and the connection was the fact that Steven Spielberg actually made the movie *Schindler's List* that inspired us and made us interested in the Holocaust. Although we were able to meet these phenomenal people, we still seem to be a bit unsatisfied, especially me. I wanted to know if these people were real from the Anne Frank diary. I wanted to know that there were no fake characters in this book. So once again, we were back on, a student said, "Ms. Gruwell, why don't we bring someone from the Anne Frank diary?"

"Oh, I'm sure all of those people are deceased," she responded. Later through research, Ms. Gruwell realized that there was a surviving member that was involved in the Anne Frank diary. It was no other than Miep Gies. The woman that actually hid Anne Frank and her family! This was a woman that I wanted to meet more than anyone. Her story was nothing less than amazing. She did whatever she had to do to help Otto Frank and his family.

I learned a lot from Miep. She taught me something that I thought I had all along, courage. The way she stood up to the Nazi soldiers as they came to find out if any Jews were in the place that the attic was located. They offered her bribes to tell on any Jews that she knew were hiding and for her not to tell was amazing. It even got so bad to the point where she was even threatened at gunpoint and she still stood firm. *Wow… what courage for one woman to possess.* We were able to get Miep to come to Long Beach as it was a big deal. The even bigger deal to me was that I was able to personally escort her into the room.

As I heard her tell her story personally, I began to fill convicted inside. I felt like I was fronting, acting like I am a good person, when I really am not. *Darrius, you are still a gang member and drug dealer*, I thought to myself. Then I thought, *You still have friends that kill people for a living.* I hung my head for a second, yet the things she stated were so inspiring that I lifted my head, raise my hand, and I said, "You are my hero."

She then looked my way and said, "No, my friend, you are the heroes." From that moment forward, the baton had been passed from her to me. That then made me realize that no matter what, I must stand for what is right and do my best to not do wrong. Now I know what I have to do. I have to leave the gang and streets alone. I have to prove that I really changed my life even if it takes my life. Thanks, Miep.

Moment of Truth

After all of these wonderful things had happened, I began to really fight within my mind of how I was going to tell these guys from my gang that I was finished. Every day as I walked home, I was stopped by them, and they would ask me why I didn't kick it with them anymore. My response differed every time I encounter them. I would say things like *"I'm spending more time at church"* or *"I am getting out of football practice late."* I even lied and said one time that *I had a kid on the way and I am trying to make a new life for him or her.* Yet there was one piece of advice that my father provided to me that I never forgot. He said, "Darrius, one day you are gone have to stand up and be a man and someone will test your manhood. At that time, you will have to show them who you really are."

I remembered that advice for the rest of my life. So I took it upon myself to take that advice to heart and implement it. I had a girlfriend at that time, and a friend of mine named Allen decided to ask me to go with him down by where my girlfriend lives. It was a stupid move. But I thought with him being my friend, it was no big deal. I found out that he and my girlfriend went to the same school. Later, she told me that many times he tried to hit on her, including this time. We went by her house, and from what I found out later. she told me that he tried to kiss her. As we were on our way home, he knew that I usually take the long way to my house instead of the short way, which is where the gang kicks it. As the bus stops at the short route that I usually took before I considered myself out of the gang, Allen got up to get off the bus and looked back, saying, "You're not going to get off?" I responded, "No, I'll take the long way."

"Come on," he said. "Stop being a punk." Now after calling me out a punk on the bus, I decided that I wasn't going to let him make me look like that, so I got up and got off the bus.

As we began to walk down the street, sure enough, I see the pack walking my way. Now the moment of truth has arrived; what do I do? Do I tell another lie, or do I take my father's advice and man up? The choice was clear with my father's voice in my head and the thought of the heroics of Miep on my mind. I continued to walk their way. "Oh, look who we have here." "What's up, Snipe?" one of the guys said. "What's up?" I replied. "Why you don't kick it any more, cuz?" *Why do they keep asking me the same question over and over?* I started to think.

Then another member walked up to me and asked, "So you not from the hood anymore or something?" while another yelled, "This nigga think he too good." As they began to gang up on me, I started to think of other excuses for not coming around so that I can keep myself safe yet only one resolution continued to come to my mind. Man up and tell the truth. "Look, I said. This isn't me. I'm just not with this anymore." As soon as I thought I would have the opportunity to give this life-changing monologue of how I want to change and be different, I was suckerpunched (*socked in the face*) from the blindside. Honestly, I thought this whole thing would happen so differently when we watch movies and someone decides to leave a gang, crew, or group. Usually, they say what they have to say and walk away with the end credits playing.

Not me, I was fighting for my life as it seemed as they were really trying to kill me. All I could think about was when I was younger and my brother was telling me that the only way out of the gang is to die out. In the midst of fighting. I felt a sharp object stick me in my upper right eye. Quickly, I jerked my head to the left and felt a rip or tearing sensation. After, the guys from the gang I was fighting against as well as people passing by on the streets suddenly stopped and stared at me like a monster. I then looked down and saw blood on my shirt, hands, and pants. I went down the street to my mother's house and knocked on the door. My mother came to the door, as she opened it, she gasped and screamed with much alarm. She tried to wipe the blood off my face, but I would not stop bleeding. The towel she tried to use filled with blood and drenched it as if I was a man-made water fountain pumping nothing but dyed red water all over the place.

As we went to the hospital, the doctors sewed me up (*applied stitches*) and told my mother and I that I am very lucky. Whatever object I was stabbed with, if it had gone any deeper, I would have been permanently blind in my right eye. From that point forward, I consider myself out of the gang. When my family members as well as others that I knew found out about this, they wanted to retaliate on my behalf. Honestly, as much as I would have liked to do something like that, I realize that this was my true test of change. I recognized that change also comes with tolerance because in order to change yourself, there are some things that you have to tolerate that you never really tolerated before your transformation. Thus, showing confirmation that your change is real. I told my family as well as associates to not do anything. From that point forward, I knew what it was like to be a new person. I realized that change is more than just a mind-set but a way of life.

Toast to Change

After all of the things that had happened, I believe Ms. Gruwell decided that we all needed some type of change. It doesn't mean that we were all bad people that needed to change to be good people. It meant that we were to change our situations. We were going to change our environments. As well as we could even change who we hung around. Therefore, I began to watch my friends and who I could call a friend. I didn't trust anybody. This is when I got the opportunity to meet Chad. He and I became very cool because he was really into music. I was into music also. Jones and I, plus a bunch of other students would congregate at lunch time and have a cipher (*standing in a circle creating music*) and we would freestyle about anything.

For me, I would rap about things that are currently happening such as how I feel, my living situation, my love life, my lack of wanting to be at school. But my claim to fame I would say was one day when Chad asked me to freestyle in front of Ms. Gruwell. I began to freestyle, and Chad would give me a word and I would freestyle using that word, and one of the words that came up was the name of my ex-girlfriend Metri. So I said a rhyme about how scandalous she was and everyone loved it.

From that point on, Chad and I began to hang out a lot. Some called us the modern-day Jimmy Jam and Terry Lewis. Once Ms. Gruwell gathered us together in our class, the room was filled with apple cider and plastic champagne glasses. She let us know that we were going to make a toast. A toast to change. On that day, I found out about a lot of the other students, but one thing I did not know or even have an idea of was the fact that Chad had been homeless. When I found that out about Chad, I think we had become closer than anyone I have ever been close to in my classroom. The reason why we were close is because I felt Chad and Jones understood me. After hearing Chad's story of homelessness, I decided that my toast was going to be a toast to a new life.

I went through the hard life, the drug dealing, and the missing father. I went through the homelessness, and I didn't want to take any more. I wanted to succeed in school and stop getting all Fs and turn them into all As. I realized those goals were obtainable if I just believed, was tolerant, listened, and applied myself. There were many others that made a toast as well. The speeches the others students in my class made were definitely inspiring. I believe we all inspired each other as well as encouraged ourselves. From that point forward, the totals for change in my eyes went down into history as the point where we all realized at the same time that we wanted better and we will receive better. It's really funny because I remember myself thinking, *Gee, is it really this simple?* But it's not. I realize by-and-by that with time and hard work, I can and will be whatever I want to be.

After the toast for change, Ms. Gruwell began to show us these black and grayish journal books. She told us just as Zlata and Anne Frank had their diaries, now we have ours. She would tell us that we don't necessarily have to write anything about ourselves. We can just do a free write, so for the first couple of times I did just that, I did a free write. She also opened it up for us to share. When she asked me what I wrote, I never wanted to share. The reason why I did not want to share was because I didn't want anyone in my business, so I would write the first thing that comes to my head. Be it that I found myself to be hungry most of the time. I would write the first thing to come to my mind like pizza, Pepsi, then pizza, and Pepsi again. So one day, she asked me to read what I wrote. Again, I gracefully bowed out, saying, "No, that's okay." She then said, "Come on, Darrius, let's hear what you got." So I mustered up enough courage to read what I wrote. Pizza, Pepsi, pizza, Pepsi. The class began to laugh, yet with Ms. Gruwell she seized every moment to make it a teachable moment.

"So, Darrius, why did you write nothing but food items?" I responded, "I don't know." The class laughed again. "But it is interesting that out of everything in the world that you could've written about, you wrote about food. So what made you write about that?" "Well," I said, "I guess I am hungry." She then responded by saying, "Okay, I get that so why are you hungry?" And I said, "Because I didn't eat." And she asked me, "Why didn't you eat?" "Because I wake up early and don't have time to eat." I said. "Well, why you didn't eat at lunch?" I dropped my head a bit and said, "I don't have money." From that point forward, she used what I wrote as a lesson. A lesson of how can a kid come to school and effectively learn if he hasn't even had breakfast or any other type of food to nurse them through the day. Ms Gruwell was amazing as most teachers would have used that as a moment to embarrass me and ship me off to detention. Yet Ms. Gruwell used it as a moment to teach us all.

Journal for Life

The more we journal, the more serious it had gotten. Various stories were read by different students that made me, along with other students, begin to write about more real things. Like being poor, being shot at, and having friends die. I was also able to open up more and found writing as a safe haven for me to be expressive of my feelings and emotions. I began to write lyrics, short stories, as well as poems because there was so much stored inside of me that needed to be released. I also see it as an opportunity to become an entrepreneur. I remember sitting at my desk, and there was a girl that I was interested in; as a matter of fact, the girl was Mela. I never had the courage to admit my young infatuations or confess to her; therefore, I would write poems.

One day, one of the guys that I actually played football with walked by my desk and saw what I was writing. He then asked me, "Hey, what are you doing?" I responded, "None of your business." He then snatched the paper away and read my poem. He began to nod his head in agreement to the things that I wrote in the poem. He asked if he could borrow it. I then asked him what for? He stated that he wanted to give it to his girlfriend. After saying no a couple of dozen times, he then asked me if he could pay me for my poem. I agreed. So I guess from that point on, you can say that I was a published poet. After that, a few more guys from my football team caught a hold of my poetry bandwagon and began to pay me to write their girlfriends' love letters as well as poems. From that point on, I developed a love for writing but not a passion.

After some time of writing in our journals, Ms. Gruwell decided that we should try to take our writings to the next level. We actually decided to try to put a book together on our own by combining our stories and giving them to the young people in our communities. I was all for the idea because I felt that these young people needed it. I know if I knew that someone was going through the same thing that I was going through, it would have made me feel a lot more at ease to know that we share the same pain. Once we wrote our stories and put them together, we began to go to different schools in our area and help within the community. But what was to come next would totally blow anyone's mind as Ms. Gruwell had an announcement. "We have reached out to our community, and now it is time to reach out another way as we are going to take a copy of our book to someone that can help change the realities that we are currently facing with education." Now hearing that made me ultimately wonder what was our Magic School Bus teacher Ms. Gruwell up to now?

Before anyone could ask her what she was talking about, she announced that all 150 of us were going to Washington, DC, to give a bound copy of our book to the secretary of education, Richard Riley. Time had passed, and we did various fund-raisers so that we can raise the money to go to Washington. While in the midst of doing all of this, we still were learning new things in Ms. Gruwell's class that taught us and prepared us for our trip to Washington as well as what we were representing, although it seemed like this would be a vacation for us. It was more like a mission that we worked hard to accomplish, as anyone knows 150 plane tickets were not cheap, and we did all we could to raise the money to go from putting change in a five-gallon water jug to throwing our own benefit concert. It was so amazing to realize that some of us have never been out of our neighborhoods, let alone out of our state. As we continued to try to raise money, a technology company CEO by the name of John Tu had stepped into the picture and did things for us that my own father has not done for me. First order of business was that he donated thirty-five brand-new computers for our classroom so that we can type our journals as well as do our homework instead of having to write them by hand. Once we graduated, Mr. Tu decided whoever graduated with the highest GPA will be able to take a computer home with them. Second, after doing that, we realized that we were only halfway to our goal of what was needed in order to pay for us to go to Washington, DC. So being the kind person that Mr. Tu is, he went ahead and took care of the other half of what it would cost to get to Washington, DC. So it was now official that we were going to take our book to Washington as we had dreamed. Thank you, Mr. Tu.

Football & Family

Football was a big deal to me. Since I had a second chance after being arrested, I really wanted to make a good impression as me staying here was riding on how I did on the field as well as in the classroom. I had friends that I would hang out with like my buddy Dip or Qwen. They were cool guys, and we all worked hard. I knew we had a big game coming up where our families could come out and be part of the festivities. I tried to get my mother to come, and every time I talked to her about it, she would say we would see. I guess that was better than no. I hyped myself up to think that she was coming. All other games were very sad for me because if I did make a good play, I would look into the stands and nobody was there to cheer me on except for my friends' parents.

During my time at practice, I would give 100 percent to what my assignment was. That didn't make my coach too proud. He would always get upset and say, "Goddamit, Darrius, stop sacking the goddamn quarterback." I was just doing my best to show I was the man for the job. Although I had enough skill, I was overshadowed by the school star that played the same position. I wanted to be better than him. I wanted to be seen. I would work out hard and go home and work out even more. I just was not getting over the hump. There were a few upperclassmen that I noticed always did well. I began to try and hang with them.

As we were in the locker room, we all were sitting around, and I saw one of the guys take this big horse pill. I asked what it was. He responded that it was something to help when losing weight. I asked if I could try it and he told me no. I kept inquiring over and over again until he finally broke. He gave me a pill and I took it. No big deal. As I continued taking the pill and training, I felt more powerful. I began lifting more weights. I felt rushes of energy. I felt honestly like I could lift a truck. People began to notice me. I began to get a little game time. The parent night game came up, and I was ready. We were hyped, and I was ready to go to war. Everybody's parents came that game. When I looked into the stand as they called our parents down to take photos with us, my mother did not come.

Again, I felt let down until I heard a voice. "Darrius, "the voice said. I looked behind me and it was my sister Patrice. That was one of the happiest moments of my life. I admit I didn't play much that game but when I did get in I did my best to show I could play. When I looked into the stands, I saw more familiar faces— my oldest brother Darryl, my sister Patrice, and brother-in-law John. From that day forward I was glad that my family came to my game, though we weren't the closest. I realized that I will always have family. Later, I realized those pills that I had taken were more than what I thought they were. They were a form of steroids the guys called Var (short for a steroid called Anavar). As soon as I recognized that, I continued taking them because I liked the way I felt and looked. I lost the weight and the guys wanted to workout with me, and we would challenge each other to get stronger and faster. But when I found out about how steroids can hurt you, I grew weary. I watched a video in health class about a football player name Lyle Alzado that died of a brain tumor in 1992 stemming from his steroid use. I left them alone but had always looked back from time to time thinking about taking Var again. In doing that, I realized the sacrifices people are willing to make to keep people loving them. I was no different. Yet I had been through too much on the streets to allow drugs or sports enhancement drugs to take my life.

After the season had ended, I began to train, knowing that the following year would be my year as the star player that played my position would be graduating. I left the guys that introduced me to the steroids alone and began to make new friends that played on the team; friends that I would have for life, Keron and Steve.

What's Our Name?

As we prepared for our trip to Washington, Ms. Gruwell provided other lesson plans which taught about history and tolerance. We began to watch *Eyes on the Prize*, which was a documentary series about the African-American Civil Rights Movement. While watching the documentary, I started to think of someone who was very dear to me, my mother, who told me stories about that time.

She would tell me how bad it was where she grew up in Mobile, Alabama. She told me the horror stories of how she was very thirsty and wanted a drink of water, but could not get a drink because it was a "White Only" water fountain. She said that when they went to the movies, the white people would be able to go into the movies the normal way, but the blacks would have to go upstairs into the balcony to watch the movies, even though they both paid the same price for entry. She told me how people were beaten and sometimes strung up just for looking at a woman who was white. Aside from my attitude, I know I would have died because the saddest part about the whole scenario is that there were people who were racist against their own race. My mother would tell me stories about how she was treated differently by people who were the same race as she was because she was not light-skinned like some of her sisters. She even told me about a time when she was very disrespectful to someone who demanded respect yet was treating her disrespectfully. And instead of my grandfather, her father, taking her side, she said that he strung her up, and she was choking and could not get air. She told me that it got so bad that it seemed that her eyes were going to pop out of her head.

As I watched this documentary, I thought solely of my mother and what she had gone through. As it continued, we began to identify with this group of young activists who called themselves Freedom Riders. Now the Freedom Riders were civil rights activists who rode buses into the segregated southern part of the United States in 1961 to test the United States Supreme Court. From reading about the Freedom Riders, I learned that the *Boynton* ruling outlawed racism in the restaurants, in waiting rooms, and in terminals serving buses that crossed state lines.

Five years prior to the *Boynton* ruling, the Interstate Commerce Commission had issued a ruling that had explicitly denounced the *Plessy v. Ferguson* doctrine of separate but equal in interstate bus travel. The authorities failed to enforce its ruling, and Jim Crow travel laws remained in force throughout the South. The Freedom Riders challenged this by riding various forms of public transportation in the South to challenge local laws or customs that enforced segregation.

What also caught our attention was that their first freedom ride started in Washington, DC. The similarity was that our message of hope and tolerance was starting in Washington, DC. They all stood up for something as well as each other. Just as we were now standing up for something we believed in as well as standing up for one another. From that point on, we realized that everything we did meant something. Everything we do in the future will matter, and it will have a name attached to it. Because we are writing to change our neighborhoods around us. It would only be fitting to take this group of 150 boys and girls that are Black, Caucasian, Hispanic, Asian, gay, straight, or any other sexual orientation, and give them a title that's so fitting for their work, dedication, and talents. We rightfully called ourselves Freedom Writers. This led us to our destiny as we finally found a name for the compilation of diary entries that we bound together to title it *An American Diary*, voices of an undeclared war.

From FW to DC

The time has finally arrived for us to go to Washington, DC. We've had meetings that included our parents as well as gatherings to fill us in on information about this trip, but now the moment is here. I can't believe it. Some of us have never even been out of Long Beach, and now we were going to Washington, DC. Part of me is anxious, while the other part is nervous. I couldn't wait to go. Beyond everything else that Mr. Tu had done for us, we arrived at the airport to find out that he has chartered an airplane for us to go to Washington, DC. The airplane was amazing. As the plane took off, I looked out the window. The plane began to go faster and faster. The nose of the plane lifted as the back of the plane followed. I realized that we were airborne so I looked back at the airport, and as we flew higher and higher, the airport along with everything else began to look smaller and smaller. Although I knew I was coming back, it felt like I was leaving for good as I looked back at my city and waved good-bye to Los Angeles.

As the plane began to land, the "Fasten Seat Belt" light came on, and everyone became silent. I was praying the plane landed safely, but I never thought of the possibility of us crashing or anything else bad happening. As the plane landed safely, we all let out an abrupt cheer. "We made it," someone said. As we exited the plane, we stepped out onto the terminal and realized we're in Washington, DC. We then went to the Marriot Hotel to check into our rooms. There were chaperones and they met with us. We reviewed our itinerary and got dressed for the events planned.

The following days were full of trips and events throughout Washington, DC. I was so inspired by our trip to the Arlington National Cemetery that I decided to journal about it. I just had the question in my mind of why it is that only people who are considered famous are the ones who get noticed. Yet when my father and friends died, nobody even knew or even cared. I hope that one day when my time to die comes that I could be immortalized with an eternal flame just as Mr. Kennedy. I never really thought about my death, yet I realize while walking through this cemetery that life and death are the only two things that are definite. I just hope that when I do die that I can leave a legacy for my family, friends, and if I am ever famous, my fans.

It would be nice to be put to rest with a twenty-one gun salute, maybe an American flag, and the hearts and condolences of billions of people. A release of doves and a horse and carriage ride through my old town that I've grown up in. I hope the memories of me will be that of grace and goodness that are nothing but pleasant stories of the kind of person that I was. When my father died, there was nothing but joking and heckling of my father owing money. Even if I didn't get any of those things I previously stated, I really hope that I could at least get a headstone. When my dad died, he didn't have a headstone, and when you go to the cemetery, you have to get a map to find where he is locate. The reason why I would want a headstone is because if I ever had any kids, they could at least find out where I am buried. I can truly say that my dad died without honor, and I don't want to die like that.

Ms. Gruwell came up with a great idea. She decided that since we all have had someone die, we should remember them when we have our candlelight vigil. Therefore, she decided that we should place the names of every friend who died on a button. I guess you can say I was the most "fashionable" as each button represented one friend or family member that has passed away. My shirt as well as the vest I had on had over thirty-five buttons that displayed the names of people that had died in my sixteen years of life. While thinking of the things that we went through as a group, I began to realize that beyond the family that I felt I didn't have, I gained a new family. Thus influencing me to write the poem "Innocent Freedom Writer," which I had the opportunity to read out loud to the secretary of education, Richard Riley.

It was a very magical night during the vigil and presentation to Mr. Riley, yet the day was not finished. The floor was cleared, and there was a DJ provided and the Freedom Writers did what we did best, we partied the night away. I will never forget this night as it was magical, emotional, and inspirational. I then realized what we were really here for and what the future held for us as freedom writers. As we walked through the streets with our hands joined together to form a chain, a guy stuck his head out of the window, asking, "Hey, what the hell are you guys doing?" And a freedom writer said it best when he replied, "We're changing the world."

Lose a Life...Lose a Legend

For some reason I had gotten very sick for the remainder of the trip, but there were some things that I had to get off the bus for and encounter. It was raining, and we got off the bus to go to the Lincoln Memorial. I remember sitting in front of it waiting for Mr. Abraham Lincoln to talk to me like I had seen him do on cartoons. It's a really huge statue to look at in person. I was unable to go to the White House because of me being sick but I did get to see things around it. You would think that everyone would be so patriotic, being that this is the capital, but instead there were swastikas directly across the street from the White House. When you look behind the White House, homelessness is right there.

Since I was sick for the duration of the trip, I was ready to go home. We had a great and very magical time. I will never forget our trip to Washington. I know that one day I want to come back and experience the things that I didn't get to experience when I got sick, like going to the White House and the Jefferson Memorial. Our good-bye to Washington was bittersweet as I know that many of us missed our home. We gathered at the airport, boarded the plane, and took off. Though we will always be in the moment of our time in Washington, DC, I know there is a nice bed waiting for me in Carson, California. Once we reached Los

Angeles International Airport, I, just like Dorothy in the *Wizard of Oz,* realized there was no place like home.

As we returned to school, we were still on a high from our trip. Yet that high started to change as we found out about a couple of students from Wilson that were charged with the rape and murder of a little seven year old black girl named Sherrice Iverson near Las Vegas, Nevada, over the weekend. When I found out about the little girl, my heart went out to her family. I realized that one of the students involved was a teammate from my football team. I didn't think he would be part of something like this as he was a good guy, a real quiet guy. I guess I was right to an extent as it was later found out that he was not the person that did the crime, yet he was an accessory. Because of what had happened, freedom writers as a whole decided we should do something about this. So we all gathered outside and around the whole school holding hands and saying prayers for the young girl and her family.

As we were standing out there, it was more on my mind than just the little girl. It was everyone that I knew personally that had been raped and killed. All I could think about was how sad it is that people have lost their lives at a young age. When you think of what it is we are losing as well as what the world is losing, it's probably the next entertainer, the next doctor to cure cancer. But by this person dying, the world will never know what they could be or could have become. I hope that one day the world can realize that every time someone dies, we lose another important life.

Therefore, I hope from this situation people who make the decision to be selfless or even selfish that they may be taking the lives of the people or person that will save their life or even the world.

First Love

High school can be considered as a great experience to almost everyone. Yet one cannot go through life without encountering a first love. In the past, the girls I have dated before, including Metri, were situations that I considered as learning lessons. At this time, being a freedom writer and spending a lot of time in room 203 to me was like a safe haven for those that have been through a lot. From our trip to Washington, we had all became friends and more like a family as we would all congregate at lunch in room 203. As I played football, I began to notice this girl that stole my heart named Stacy. Stacy was beautiful to me as well as she was just so cool. I must say she was another crack into the hardness of my heart that made a way for true love and trust to find its way to the outside of my heart.

She would wait for me after school for me to get out of football practice, or sometimes I would wait for her to get out of gymnastics. We would talk on the phone, but mostly in person enjoying each other's company. At times I'd stare into the distance, maybe dreaming or just simply wondering about my situation, and she would look at me as if she already knew what I was thinking. When she didn't know what I was thinking, she would simply ask me. She was one of my best friends. In a world full of noise, she was my mute button to it all. When we were together, nothing else mattered. Sometimes I even had to admit that she may have saved me from myself. The reason I say that is because the time I spent with her probably took from the time I would have spent getting in trouble. I recognized that I began to feel more for this girl. I would walk her home or come to her house on the weekend to hangout and watch television.

I always wondered why I got the opportunity to meet her mom but not her stepdad. One day, I found out. As we were hanging out as usual, he came home drunk or maybe even high, but he was not too coherent to what was going on. He began to get violent and I was asked to go home. From that point on, I was worried about her living in that house. I know it had to be more going on than what I seen. On my bus ride home I thought about Stacey and began to think about the crackhead's daughter that was offered to me for drugs. So since I couldn't save her, I would do things to try and keep her out of the house for as much time as possible. When she had to go home, I was sad to see her go because I knew that her being home gave her stepfather a greater chance to hurt her. I remembered how good it felt to be part of room 203, so I invited her to come to the classroom with me. She had come around before when we all went on a field trip to Medieval Times, and Ms. Gruwell allowed me to invite her, but we were just friends at that time.

I really pushed her to join our class. She tried to join it, but she couldn't join until next year. Ms Gruwell finally found a way to get her into the class before the school year was out. She finally got the opportunity to be in the class, and I was so excited. She began attending class, and we let it be known that we were a couple. We went everywhere together. I began to feel more and more things for her. I think I'm in love. But how can I be in love when I don't even know what love is? I never confessed that to my buddies though. Yet a situation happened to show the whole school where my heart lies.

Stacy and I would talk about everything together, and one day, she showed up at school, telling me that she had a dream. She said the dream was about my friend Jay. I asked her to expound more on the dream, and she wouldn't tell me the rest. The fact that she was dreaming about a friend of mine bothered me for most of the day. As I was in class, I told Jay about what Stacy had said. He then laughed. I asked what he was laughing about, and he stated that she was dreaming about him because they had been intimate before. When that was said, I began to laugh it off. He then said, "No, I'm serious. We did have sex." I began to feel a fire of anger erupt inside of me. My heart dropped to my feet, and I couldn't believe what I was hearing.

I waited until lunch, and I asked Stacy what was the dream about. She would not tell me. I drilled her again, asking what the dream was about. She finally broke her silence and said that it was a sexual dream. I got even more upset. I then decided to ask her the question that started all of this. "Did you guys really have sex?" She then replied, "No." I couldn't believe it. I called Jay my friend and he lied to me. I felt really betrayed as I ran up the stairs to the science building with rage. Soon as I got to the third floor, I saw him and screamed his name. "Jay!" Soon as he turned and said hey, I grabbed him by his shirt and held him against the rail with his body hanging halfway over. "Why'd you lie?" I said. He then said, "What?" "Why did you lie to me, Jay?" I said. As he was trying to explain, Stacy ran upstairs with her friend, begging me to let him go. The crowd grew thick and my friends that I played football with, Keron and Steve, pulled me off him and rushed me away from the scene. Later, Jay apologized to me and Stacy. He said that it was a mistake, and he was sorry for lying. From that point on, I realized that you can't trust what people say. Stacy and I had a good relationship, yet our differences brought us to an abrupt end. Finishing the year out, I was worried about what would happen with me and her both being part of the freedom writer group. It bothered me to be around her and know we were not together. Ah, young love.

I remember just wishing over and over again that she would not be there or that we just wouldn't be around each other. My wish became true as one day I came to school and she wasn't there. I went to her house and no one was there. It was like she had vanished. I never saw her again to let her know what I had finally realized. That she is my first love. Until the end of the school year, I found myself waiting for her to come back so I could tell her how I felt, but she never showed back up. As the summer approached, I spent most of my time working my first job at the Long Beach Health Department as I basically kept myself as busy as I could to keep myself out of trouble. I dropped out of football because I had gotten injured the year before, and I had discovered my new hobby: girls. I spent a lot of time journaling as well. It kept me sane and able to process my thoughts more logically because they were on paper. I wrote a lot in my journal. I wrote a lot of poems that were about love, life, and luxury as well as the three things that I loved most: my mom, Stacy, and the freedom writers.

Superstar

I returned to Woodrow Wilson High School for my senior year; time surely flew fast. Besides elementary school, this is the longest I have stayed at one school. It's going to be good to see my friends and my new found freedom writer family. I'm hoping Stacy shows up as I still want to tell her how I feel. I can't believe Ms. Gruwell has gotten to keep us all the years I have been here. I can't believe I made it to my senior year. I mean I didn't think I was going to live to see sixteen, and here I am. I came in as a drug dealer and walking out a scholar. Standing here at the front of the school, it no longer looks like a college to me. It actually seems small now. Though everyone will be hanging out this year, I will have to play makeup since I didn't do too well until I started really applying myself in Ms. Gruwell's class and changing my ways. Being a freedom writer influenced me to do better in my other classes as well. My counselor said that I am behind in credits. So if I do the zero periods, an after-school class and participate in the work experience class that meets at lunch, then I will be in line to do something my father and brother didn't get the opportunity to do. Graduate.

Now that the freedom writers were well-known in our school, there were many students that wanted to be part of our group. By this time, we had been to Washington D.C and won multiple awards such as the Crystal Apple Award. Ms. Gruwell and the freedom writers had become a household name. Once we hit our senior year, everyone's focus began to be on prom and graduation. Since my mother heard about me graduating, she was so excited. Seeing her excited made me very happy. She told my whole family that I was graduating, and they were all getting together to try and buy me a car as well as help her do whatever was needed for me to have a wonderful prom and graduation. Man, life is truly great. I never thought that this could happen to me. I am very excited. As the freedom writers continued to chalk up awards and contribute to our community, we found out that Connie Chung wanted to do a piece for primetime live on the freedom writers. We were all excited about that. I loved the way things were going. You can say for the first time, I felt the most wonderful high without using drugs. I felt I had a future now. I'm looking at colleges and everything. I figured that since I had a lot of trouble out here maybe I can try to get in at Morehouse, Howard, or Tuskegee. Then I thought about shooting for the stars and trying to get in to my all-time favorite college choice USC. As well as I had the love and respect of people that I thought I could never earn it from. My family.

I know I used to feel depressed a lot, but if this is what life can offer me, I surely want to live it to the fullest. I'm glad for all the things that are happening as I never thought that it could be this good. Ms. Gruwell had also made an announcement that Connie Chung was coming to our class to interview us for Primetime Live. When she came out, we all had a great time and did what we usually do. We displayed our freedom writer magic. See, with freedom writer magic, it's infectious. What freedom writer magic is I would describe as us spreading imaginary magic pixie dust around a room, bearing hope and happiness with our laughs, music, and voices. We would have many times of gathering together, singing songs like "Lean on Me," "Stand by Me," etc. We would dance and lip-synch our favorite songs and just have an all-out good time. Nothing but smiles here when we are together. I love the freedom writers and I know they love me. When we have freedom writer magic, it brings us all together as a family, a freedom writer family.

Darrius vs. Darrius

S ometimes, when I look at life, I realize the rollercoaster effect that I am constantly taken on. Every time that I have been up, something has always happened to pull me down. As we continued to speak at elementary schools and other places as freedom writers, more and more people began to know who we were, especially people like Jones, Ava, and I. As I was in one of my classes, I was summoned to the counselor's office. She gave me some information that completely took the wind out of my sails of happiness. My counselor called me in her office and was telling me how proud she was of my progress. Although her appreciation was welcomed, I knew I was there for another reason.

As she prepared to tell me what was wrong, she took a deep breath and began to say that she is sorry. I asked her, "What's wrong?" She proceeded, saying, "Darrius, I know I told you that if you took advantage of the programs that you are in now such as your zero period and work study and after-school programs that you would graduate. But—" As she started to say the rest, I stopped her, asking, "What does this mean?" She then said the words that are probably the scariest words that I would hear from someone besides a doctor admitting I had a terminal illness. She said, "Darrius, you are not going to graduate. Your credits are too far behind." My heart dropped to my feet, and my eyes began to well up with tears. I ran out of the office, sobbed, and cried over and over again. When I mustered up the courage, I called my mother and told her the news.

When I told my mother, I thought she would say what any other mother would say, telling their child "it's okay" or "things will work out." But she then turned on the same tough love she used on me during the time I was on the street. She said, "See, Darrius, I knew you couldn't do right. You have me telling everyone you're going to graduate and you're not? When you get home, I want you to get your stuff and go. You have been playing games all along." To hear her say that, I was heartbroken. I had totally forgotten about not graduating because something much worse had happened to me. Once again, I disappointed my mother.

Days passed, and I was still trying to cope with the news of not graduating as well as wondering where I was going to sleep. I began to stay with different friends like my boy Keron, Chad, and even spent a few nights at Jones's house. I was tired of being a disappointment and wanted to just end it all. Suicide kicked was around in my mind constantly, like a soccer star practicing alone. I figured that I was tired of being a failure and that's all I am going to be. I was too embarrassed to admit to Ms. Gruwell that I was not going to graduate as well as tell her that I'm homeless again. I remembered my chaperone from my trip to Washington, Cottrell. I talked to him, and he allowed me to stay with him for a little while. I began to go on a downward spiral. I started smoking weed again. I didn't care too much about anything or anybody. My feelings of inner darkness invaded my thoughts and blocked my hopes and dreams of going to college like dark clouds block the sun.

I continued down this path until an incident occurred that allowed me to prove to myself that I couldn't do the drugs anymore. I lashed out in class when I felt the students were disrespecting Ms. Gruwell by over talking her and not paying attention when she was trying to teach. I walked up and wrote Disneyland on the chalkboard and hit the chalkboard as I said, "That's what you assholes think this is, huh?" And I walked out of the class. I was in rage, and I ran into the bathroom and began to cry again. I went to the sink to wash my face and hands. I looked up at the mirror as I washed my hands, and in the mirror, I finally saw the guy my mother would get mad at and talk mess to when she saw me. It was my father. I got so pissed at what I saw that I turned my head to hide my face and snatched up the sink that I was washing my hands in and pulled the sink out the wall and threw it. Though I left it alone, I felt the same adrenaline rush and strength I would feel from taking the steroids. Again, the monster had come out. At that moment, I realized that all this time I have been running, it wasn't from my father, my mother, or anybody else. I was running from myself. At that moment, I realized that I had to start loving myself and dealing with what's at hand no matter what the problem is and stop feeling sorry for myself and most of all be responsible, starting with admitting to Ms. Gruwell who broke the sink.

As I walked back into the class, I apologized to everyone for my lash out and admitted to Ms. Gruwell about the broken sink. She knew that if the broken sink was brought up to administration that I would be kicked out of the school, just like I had been kicked out of other schools, but she helped me stay there. I had been fighting against myself all along, and through that experience, I figured how to love myself and others and because of the love that I had for myself, I should never want to hurt or kill myself because I realized that you never hurt the ones you love. Therefore, I vowed to love myself and never entertain the thought of suicide or hurting myself ever again.

Homeless Habits

As I line up for my name to be called for graduation, I slowly pan around the stadium. I saw and heard the cheers from my fellow peers and their parents. Everyone is clapping, waving their hands, and blowing noisemakers. As I walk up the stairs to the stage, I heard the principal say, "Our next graduate is Darrius Garrett." I got happier and happier as I began to walk across the stage toward the principal. I looked to the left at the seat I know my mother would be in and my mother was not there. As I began to shake the principal's hand and reach for my diploma, I then woke up. I realized that it was all a dream. I look around the room, and I am in Cottrell's living room on the couch. As I lay down to fall back to sleep, I realize it's time to go to school.

At least I'm not too far from the school now since Cottrell only lives down the street. Although I stayed at Cottrell's, I tried to move around a bit so that I wouldn't wear out my welcome. Sometimes, I would just stay out all night and try to not evade Cottrell's space. Being a Freedom Writer sometimes we forget that outside our Freedom Writer world of peace, tolerance, and harmony, that the "real world" is not so friendly. Therefore, I was ignorant to the fact that Cottrell lived in a predominately Caucasian neighborhood. So when I would go to his house, I would get looked at pretty funny as if they knew I didn't belong there. It was sad because this woman made up a story that someone tried to rape her, and it just so happened it was a chunky black dude. *Well, how convenient,* I thought to myself as I heard the story from Cottrell. So now I'm not graduating, I'm homeless, and his neighbors think I'm the Long Beach Rapist. I know that was a vague conversation, hinting to me that I have to leave, but we fought for a little longer to keep me living there.

I went on to school, and I guess my living situation will be a bit better at least for a few days as Ms. Gruwell let us know that we were going to New York to receive the Spirit of Anne Frank Award. I was very excited to go. I'm not sure who knew I was homeless at this point, but I was trying my best to hide it from everyone. Not having a place to live isn't necessarily a badge of honor to wear. So I tried to keep it as quiet as possible. As Ms. Gruwell explained to us the itinerary for our trip to New York, I thought about the fact that when we started the freedom writer movement that we didn't even plan to do things like this or win awards or anything. We just planned to change the community around us. I've only seen New York on movies like *New York Undercover* and rap videos.

I want to see the different landmarks like the Statue of Liberty, the Brooklyn Bridge, and the New York skyline. I can't wait to go. Before I left, there were a few things I needed to take care of, such as me going to my mother's and letting her know that I was leaving. When I told her, she thought I was saying that I was moving to New York. The best thing she could say to me was bye. I swear sometimes I feel like my mom just hates me. I can't imagine how a mother can just say bye to her son like that. I guess now since I'm not graduating, she sees me as a nobody just like my father. Watch, one day she will see just like everyone else. I promise. I'm going to be somebody, and she will hopefully look back at me and smile with the satisfaction that her son has made it.

New York, New York

Our trip to New York was nothing short of amazing; this was the first time I ever got to go to New York. As we landed in JFK airport, I began to get excited. The only time I got to see Times Square was on MTV and be it that I wanted to be a big-time rapper, I couldn't wait to visit places like Radio City Music Hall, Madison Square Garden, alongside other places, or maybe Jones and I will run into my idol Mr. Russell Simmons or maybe Lyor Cohen or Kevin Liles and rap for them in person and get signed to Def Jam Records. Since they already have some of my favorite rappers signed like LL Cool J, Redman, Jay-z, Run DMC, and the hometown heroes Warren G and Jayo Felony I thought why not try.

There I go with my big dreams again, I thought to myself as we stepped into the revolving doors of the Marriott that we were lodging at during our stay in New York. This Marriott was amazing as the elevators looked like space capsules shooting into the air. It really reminded me of the cartoon *The Jetsons*. This place was really classy; as we walked around the lobby, I thought to myself that this is a big difference from the Snooty Fox (*a motel in Los Angeles*). Our rooms were immaculate, and hallelujah, I had a bed to sleep in, my own bed. As I snuggled into the warm cozy bed, I felt my drive to make it and be successful grow stronger as

I drifted off to sleep. I realized that I don't ever want to be homeless again. Ever!

As we woke up and prepared for breakfast, I was thinking of the average continental juice and Danish type of food to be prepared. As we walked to the main dining area where they were serving, I was blown away. The sweet smell of orange juice peeled through the walls of the hotel, and the smell of tender sausage tickled my nose. I was really blown away when I saw that they made omelets on site, and you can tell them what you wanted on it and they would make it. Amazing! Then they would make any type of waffles you want right off the griddle. Be it that I love food, this was definitely a big deal to me. After breakfast, the festivities began. We walked around to the different places in the area and got to see places like the Rockefeller Center and the biggest toy store that was on this movie I loved starring Tom Hanks called *Big*. It was a FAO Swartz toy store. Now I don't know about anyone else, but I was so intrigued by this store. Although I had sold drugs, been shot at, saw friends die, was part of a gang, and been homeless. I will always have a soft spot for toys and video games.

As we traveled and did more sightseeing, they were loading us all on a boat. I didn't know what we were about to do or where we were going. As the boat began to move, I thought to myself, *Do I get seasick?* Well, by this time, we were in the middle of the ocean now, so I needed to just deal with it. But before I could even contemplate being sick from the boat, I saw something that I had only seen on television. I saw the thing that people in war-torn and poverty-stricken countries long to see. It was the Statue of Liberty. All I could think was *wow*.

It mean a lot to me to be able to experience seeing the Statue of Liberty because at that point, everything I had taken for granted being born and raised as a citizen of the United States made me realize that everyone isn't free and to be in a country that we can believe in who we want to believe in, love who we want to love, or have the freedom to say we don't like our president or to say fuck the police in a song without being killed for it is awesome. Granted though, people feel that things are not all great with this country, yet at this time, right now, I am proud to be an American.

Spirit of Anne Frank

Waking up in an unknown place would probably make most people uncomfortable. For me, I wanted to sleep as long as possible as it seemed as the beds in the hotels were made perfectly for me. I knew we had to get up, and it took everything for me to get out the bed. Yet it kept calling my name as I was so tired from the day before. Today's itinerary was for us to go to the Anne Frank Museum Exhibit they had displayed to accept the spirit of Anne Frank award. As we attended the ceremony for the presentation of the Spirit of Anne Frank award, there were other people from the media there, as well as a well-known actress there that I recognized. She was presenting the award. Wait, it's Alice from that show my mom used to watch when I was a kid. Well, her real name isn't Alice. That was the name of her character on the show. It was Linda Lavin. As she stood up there and presented the award to Ms. Gruwell, it was all surreal. I guess that seemed fit for her to present the award since she was doing the play *The Anne Frank Diary* on Broadway. It felt good to be non-Jewish or totally different from what Anne Frank was and still win such a wonderful award. I realized that when I get older, I definitely want to be a humanitarian and recognized, not necessarily just for my work, but just for doing what's right. Helping out others and making their lives better while leaving a legacy.

Night fell as we got the opportunity to go see an actual play on Broadway. We went to see *The Diary of Anne Frank* play, and it was a really good play. I've never been to a play before except for the plays I did for my church when I was young. I thought it worked just like the movies, but I guess not. They took like two intermissions: the first intermission I didn't know what they were doing so I was upset because I thought that was the end of the play. I remember asking everyone, "Is that it?" over and over again. After seeing the play, we got to go to the Virgin Megastore in Times Square. Being a person that loved music, I felt like I died and had gone to musical heaven. When I first walked in, I saw a DJ in the sky booth, but the concept of a live DJ in the record store was brilliant. Then there were multiple floors of music and music books and music games. I was in love. If I had money, I would have probably bought everything that I could from that store.

On our way back to the hotel, there were things that really intrigued me that I never saw at home in California. There were people performing on the street doing things like beating on the bottom of buckets making a beat. They were playing beats from the popular songs that were out on the radio. I never saw anything like that before. I guess it is true that music is all around us because the guys were beating on buckets; there was another guy doing percussion with bottles and someone else beating on a hollow-type tree branch and another guy using this thing that looked like a seashell. They had an all out band made up of items that could be found around the house. I thought to myself,

How creative. I always thought that a professional drum machine such as a MPC-3000 or keyboard like a Triton is needed to make real music like Dr. Dre when he makes a beat, but I was wrong. I figured that I could use anything around me to make music as a producer. Especially if you wanted to be innovative. Who would have thought that we could have made it to this point of just reading about Anne Frank to winning an award that commemorates her spirit? I was so proud to be a recipient.

Hey, Connie

Night fell and we were having dinner as we were invited to a special guest's room that was in the hotel. As we got in the elevator, our chaperone pressed the top button of the hotel. The P for penthouse as the elevator went up and up and up I began to think, *Wow, we are going to the place that nobody else goes.* As the door opened, it seemed like it opened up to this whole other world. There were cameras and lights in place and people walking around. As we walked in, there was this lady that everyone was talking to as she was having her makeup fixed. Oh my God, it was Connie Chung. I have seen this lady on television over and over again, and now I have the opportunity to meet her in person. The last time she came to our school I missed her because I had football practice. But now here she is in the flesh.

We began the interview, and she began to ask us questions about who we are, what we have done so far, etc. We began to talk about our time in Washington, DC, when we got to meet the secretary of Education Richard Riley. As we were talking and laughing, I stopped for a minute, and my mind began to journey back into my neighborhood. Then I thought to myself that I'm laughing and talking with big-time news anchors and seeing plays when my little friends that I had left back at home were still struggling, still homeless, and still dying. I thought about Smurf, Troy, my cousins, and my friends that had passed on, and I wanted to cry. As the interview continued, she began to ask more questions. Then I thought about how many buttons I wore that night when we were having the vigil for the people we had lost when we were in Washington DC, and internally, I began to sob.

All the questions she was asking began to take me further and further into my past and bring me back to the future. I couldn't take it. The pain was too deep and hurtful, my mind continued to run on, showing me vividly the faces of the people that I had lost. I'm trying to hold in the pain and hide it with a smile until a tear escaped my eye. Connie Chung caught it and asked, "Why are you crying, Darrius?" I had began to speak, saying, "I think about all the things that Ms. Gruwell has helped me with and how my friends are locked down or dead right now. I could have been them right now…right now 'cause I didn't have a life." As I spoke, the whole room listened; I felt nothing but embarrassment being a six-foot, 220-pound linebacker crying. After I got done spazzing out, I looked over the room. Guys and girls alike were all crying. Connie Chung had to stop the taping and redo her makeup, we all were in tears. I guess a lot of us felt the same way.

From that time forward, I realized that it was okay to cry. I wrote a poem that night, and it was just saying, *"No matter who you are, hurt blemishes our hearts as dirt blemishes the streets, and crying is the rain that washes away the hurt just as rain washes away the dirt that blemishes the streets."* Once again, we experienced a freedom writer moment. I was glad to call these people my family as I didn't want the night to end because honestly, I had a lot more crying to do but I guess it will take the rest of my life to finish crying. I was saddened that tomorrow all this will come to an end. I enjoyed myself and was exposed to a lot of things I had never been exposed to before. I can't wait for the day that I could come back to New York on my own and enjoy more of what they had to offer. I really wanted to go to Harlem, Brooklyn, or even Jersey and visit the boroughs or check out the Apollo Theater and the good food that I hear about as well as the Italian Icees that I heard Tupac talk about on his song "Nothing Like the Old School."

Hopping on the plane to go back home, I still kept my eyes peeled for stars, and I didn't get to see anyone I thought maybe as fate has it that I really wanted to see Mr. Russell Simmons, but that didn't happen either. I enjoyed this trip a lot as it really opened me up to a lot more things. I can't wait to come back to New York, but for now, I can't wait to go home. Oh wait...I have no home.

Stop and They Will Shoot

Waking up this morning, I realize that I didn't feel up to going to school. On my way to school, I ran into my buddy Don and my boy Laz and decided I felt like just hanging out. My mom accused me of ditching all my time here at Wilson anyway, so I might as well utilize my senior year to do it. Once I relayed my voice of reason to Laz and Don, they both were game (*okay*) with it. I would never try to persuade anyone to ditch school, but honestly, we had a crazy time. We were all over Long Beach, and we really enjoyed ourselves. We went to a friend's house and hung out for a bit. After, we decided that the day was getting past us and we needed to head back to school.

Before heading back, we had to make one more stop. Don had to go pick up some weed. The voice inside me had already acknowledged that this didn't seem right, but I went anyway. As we were walking down the street, we began to migrate closer and closer to my old neighborhood by the yellow apartments I grew up in on the Eastside of Long Beach. We were telling jokes and making fun of each other when this car just swerves up and two men hop out the car with nine millimeter handguns, yelling for us to get down on the ground. It was the undercover police. As I got on the ground, I noticed that Don had his hands in his jacket. As I am being handcuffed, I'm thinking to myself, *Here we go again. I'm going back to jail.* Then I thought about it and realized this time I didn't do anything. In the midst of my thoughts, I heard the yelling of the police telling Don to show his hands. He yelled he can't.

When he said that, I got scared and I knew he was about to get blown away in front of us. I looked at Laz, and Laz looked at me and we both at that time were thinking should we make a run for it or should we stay and watch Don get his brains plastered against the wall from the slugs of the 9mm that both of the undercover officers were toting. I yelled at Don, telling him, "Just put your hands up, please, man." Laz repeated the same. As Don began to open his jacket, all I saw was something black and shiny. I thought to myself he's about to shoot it out with the cops and we're going to get caught up for it. As he pulled his jacket open even more, you can see that it was something bigger than a gun. As he pulled it out of his jacket, the officers were still yelling, and I closed my eyes tight because I knew he was a dead man. There were no gunshots as I slowly opened my eyes.

It was a video game that he had stolen from the friend's house that we were hanging with. I just shook my head as I realized the same thing the officer told us. He said, "You guys almost died today over a fucking video game." They said that they stopped us because there was a robbery and shootout in the area. And the guys that did the shooting resembled us; once they checked our IDs and realized that we were supposed to be in school, they let us go and told us to stay off the streets. I think that moment was so big of a life changer for me because it showed me how one decision that you think doesn't even affect you can affect your whole life, just as Don had the video game.

He could have had a gun, and if he did have a gun, all three of us would have been shot. When I got back to the school, Laz and I stopped by Ms. Gruwell's class and got our work that she gave out to us and realized that we both were lucky to be alive that day as a sigh of relief escaped both of our chests. This will be the first and the last time I ever ditch school because it just feels like I'm cursed because every time I make a decision like this, I end up with a consequence that I have to suffer. Though it sucks, I realized that this is a lesson about life. As long as I learned from it, then it's worth the encounter.

A Family with a Big Heart

I had been in and out of different places here and there; I had finally come out and admitted to Ms. Gruwell that I was homeless. When she found out, she was appalled that I had been in this position and nobody knew. I told her about the situation of me not graduating and how disappointed my mother was; as bad as it seemed for my mother to kick me out, I began to understand because I seem to be nothing but a failure. Nothing could ever go right for me, and with all that I put her through from the age of thirteen until now, it was just too much for a parent to stand. Once Ms. Gruwell and I talked, she asked around to different freedom writers, asking if I could stay with them. I admit it was very embarrassing as everyone now knew that I didn't have a place to stay. I had already stayed at Jones's house as well as Keron house, and Cottrell's house. Now I have to stay at someone else's house. *I don't know how I am going to make it through this year*, I thought to myself.

One of the guys that I was pretty cool with raised his hand. He can come to my house. I didn't know him that well, yet all I knew was his name, which was George Ryan, one of the white guys in the class. Personally, I didn't even think that he would care enough to even allow me to go there. Or maybe even embarrassed to have a black guy in his car. I mean we had became a family as far as the freedom writers were concerned, but

I knew that stereotypes and racism still existed outside the door of room 203, and I wasn't going to be ignorant to the fact that it could still be going on and thought about within our group. I was so wrong; George Ryan is one of the coolest people you could ever meet. I mean, he is a true friend. Though George Ryan is a cool guy, it seemed like his life was good and he had not a care in the world. As he was driving to his house, he began to ask me questions about my mother, trying to understand how a parent can kick their child out of the house. On the other hand, I was wondering how a kid could get such a nice car at sixteen. The more he drove, the more nervous I got as we began to get more and more onto the good side of town. The place I knew I didn't belong.

As we pulled up to his house, I was amazed. You could fit my mother's house into this house twice. As we entered the house, I had a big culture clash as there was no yelling in the house. No arguing. I felt like I was in heaven. As time grew later, I began to hang with George Ryan and his father had arrived. I just knew his father was going to tell him that I couldn't stay solely because he didn't even ask permission. But he didn't. I'll never forget how warm and caring his father and whole family was. I honestly wanted to be adopted by this family. I saw the way that they would coexist with each other as a family.

Once his father met me, he had a long talk with me and he began to show me a bit of where my mother was coming from. I had now encountered another male that I wanted to be like. From all ends of what this man was and represented made me feel like I understood why George Ryan was so caring and giving because his father was the same way. These people took me in and didn't have any problems with doing so. Usually, you would notice people with money as snobbish and uncaring, yet that thought of rich people were kind of abolished and done away with from my interactions and meeting of Mr. John Tu.

I appreciated George Ryan's family and his dad for all they had done. Although he may have thought he helped me keep from being homeless, I would say he actually taught me a bit about being a man. I'm not saying that I would let just anyone stay with my family and me, but I know a lot of things that George Ryan's dad was all about and represented. I definitely want to be somewhat like him as he in my eyes, along with the other great men I have encountered and will encounter in my life were definitions of real men.

Good News

After a few long years of hard work and writing from the heart, we put together a book telling hideous and heart-wrenching stories to change the lives of the youth in our community. We later found out that Ms. Gruwell had another surprise for us. As we were all wandering around campus for most of the day thinking what it could possibly be, I began to get very restless. Is it another trip? Is it more donated computers? Maybe it's another trip to the Museum of Tolerance? As we went into the room where Ms. Gruwell was waiting for us, there were people standing around as we saw a camera crew and news anchor Connie Chung was there as well. I thought her visiting us again was the surprise that Ms. Gruwell had for us, but there was more in store. She then had people who were involved with us through the years come to the room as well.

This seemed like another toast for change moment as she had sparkling cider displayed, she asked that we all pick up a glass as she made the announcement that the manuscript we wrote and put together was picked up by a major publisher by the name of Doubleday/ Random House and our book was going to be published. When she told us, we were all full of joy. I didn't know what that meant exactly. I didn't know if that meant we were going to be rich, if we were going to be famous, or if we were going to finally be known as authors. What I did know is that we all put forth so much effort and time into this book. A lot of us bared our souls and did it all in hopes that we could help change the lives in our neighborhood. Now we realized that we would contribute to changing lives all over the world.

As I thought about all that we had been through together, I began to get teary eyed because a lot of us felt that we were not going to make it at one point. Now we aren't just going to have a publishing deal, but most of us are going to graduate, some were going to college, some starting their family lives, and others were going to go to the Armed Forces. I can't believe that we grew up so much in so little time. As I glanced around the room, I noticed the growth and maturity in us all. We began to see the changes in our lives that some of us looked towards being the first to graduate in their family. Some of us had the highest GPAs that we have ever had in our entire lives. I personally changed my GPA from a 0 point Grade Point Average coming in to Wilson High, to a 2.7 as a Junior barely making it to play football, and now knocking on a 3.0 as a Senior.

I realized for myself that although I'm homeless, I will still become somebody, and with the title of author under my belt, I can do anything. I don't know where we will go from here, but I do know that wherever we go, it will be pleasant. I don't know what the future will bring, but I do know my future will include me being a freedom writer and loving every minute of it.

Prom Night

Everyone was so excited about prom night except for me. I found out, If I wasn't on the list to graduate then I couldn't attend prom. People were buying tickets, making plans, and just preparing themselves for the night that every parent talks about. I knew that I couldn't go to prom, yet I got it in my mind that I could go. Guess it was a coping mechanism for not being able to attend and not being disappointed about it. Nobody knew that I wasn't graduating, plus they also didn't know that I couldn't go to prom. So my friends would talk about what type of tux they were going to wear, and I wouldn't say much. Then they would talk about who they were taking, and I would continue to be silent. As time grew closer and closer to prom, I began to calculate in my mind a couple of girls that I wanted to take. So I asked a girl named Jen, who was one of the smartest in my class; she was attractive and smart. I walked up to her, we talked for a bit, and I asked her straight out, "Would you like to go to the prom with me?" She agreed and I was happy that she was okay with going with me.

After I had made a date to go with Jen to the prom, I tried my best to figure out how I am going to get into the prom. Now that I was going with her, my mind was very set on going. Every day at school, I would ponder on ways to get there. Jen would remind me that prom is so many days away, asking if I had certain things taken care of. I would reply, "Yeah, I got that already," knowing that I didn't. Finally a way out presented itself to me. A girl that worked in the office named Lisa asked me if I was taking anyone to the prom. I responded with the only answer that made sense to get me into the prom, "No." She then said, "Well, if you aren't taking anyone, would you like to go together?" "Yes," I said. "But I don't think I could go because of my graduation status." She then said, "Don't worry about that." So cool. I'm on my way to prom…perfect; I can definitely work this out.

While on my high of knowing I can now go to prom, I began to try and find a way to pay for all of my stuff on my own. I thought of everything possible to try and get money to pay for my ticket, tux, and the rest of the stuff I needed. I had a little money because I worked for the Long Beach Health Department as a peer educator about HIV/AIDS and STDs since my dad died of AIDS. While sitting deep in thought, I was sitting next to one of the prettiest girls in school, Mella. For some reason, we began to talk about prom, and I was telling her that I wanted to go but didn't know how I was going to do it. As I was talking, she began to tell me how nobody has asked her yet. Hmm…my mind began to work like a heavy-duty machine, turning its wheel over and over again. Before my mind could register it, my mouth took over and quickly said, "I want to take you, that's why nobody asked." She then laughed. "No, I'm serious, I want to take you to prom, it'll be an honor." She then smiled and said, "Okay, sure, we can go to prom." Woohoo! I couldn't believe it, I'm about to take the prettiest girl in

school to our school prom. I can't believe it. I bragged
to my friends. I was on cloud nine. All I have to do
now is figure out how to make this all work. Over and
over again, I played it in my head on how I would work
this out. I guess when it comes down to it, I will just
do what any other guy would try to do. Take all three
girls to prom. I'm sure I would make history pulling
this off, but how?

Fate had it, somebody was a hater in my crew and
it got back to Lisa that I was attempting to take three
women to the prom. When confronted about it, I told
her that I thought we could all just go as friends. She
didn't like that one bit. Later, I realized that I was not
added to the list to go to prom like Lisa promised. I
waited as long as I could until the last minute to tell
Jen and Mela that I couldn't go. They both understood,
but as for me, I was heartbroken. I didn't mean to try
and make them feel like they weren't special. It's just
that I wanted it all at one time: prom, three smart and
beautiful girls, and to enjoy the night with my freedom
writer family, football teammates, and friends. But it
didn't go that way.

Instead, I spent my time alone with nobody around
because everyone was at prom. I then called my friend
Keron as he and Steve graduated already because they
were a year ahead of me. We got to hang out, and it was
pretty cool. I had probably a better time than I would
have had going to prom. Probably not that much fun
but after everyone got out of the prom, I received phone
call after phone call from friends and freedom writers
like Chad, asking where I was. They were letting me

know where the after prom was going to be. That felt really good because it made me know that even though I wasn't there, my presence was still felt and that I had friends that really loved me.

Graduation

The time that a lot of people waited more than seventeen years for had now arrived, graduation. It's hard to believe that something you wait so long for seems to come so quickly. I know all of my friends are very happy to have accomplished so much, yet I don't have much to be happy for at all. I am still homeless as well. I need 220 credits to graduate and I had 205. I was only fifteen credits short of graduation. Ms. Gruwell found out and did her best to get them to allow me to graduate. Since I was already kicked out of the house because of this, I didn't have much fight in me. Also, I had not purchased cap and gown or anything so I felt there was no use.

This scenario taught me a lot about family because when everyone found out that I would not graduate, including some freedom writers' parents, they reached out to assist me. I felt really good about that because it showed me how much love people had for me. I was overwhelmed. Ms. Gruwell also called out the big guns. What I mean is I even received a call from the superintendent of our school district, Dr. Carl Cohn. This man was someone I really looked up to, as the way he spoke and the way he carried himself to me was reminiscent of the dean at my middle school: Dean Kinsey. Dr. Cohn asked me what was going on. I was very embarrassed to admit that I was not graduating.

As everyone continued to get themselves together for graduation, I decided to leave as I grew more and more disappointed in myself. I began to walk to the place I call home at that time, which was Cottrell's house as he allowed me to come back to his house to finish out my school term. I even contemplated an old habit of smoking some weed just to clear my conscience and try to get my mind off what was going on. But I remembered that I changed. And no matter what, when you change whether good or bad things occur, I realize that I must stay the course and do what's right, not just for me, but for my body, so I didn't smoke.

While walking, something kept telling me to turn around and go back to Ms. Gruwell class. I didn't at that time. I just wanted to feel sorry for myself and go hide under a rock. But I wish I had gone back because I later found out that I was eligible to walk the stage. Not just that, but also my friends told me that my name was in the program for people to walk across the stage. To this day, I still think of that and get upset as it was a big deal for me to just walk across the stage because that was something that my father or brother, had not gotten the chance to do. When I found out, I quickly called my mother and told her what could have been and her thoughts of that were just as mine, thinking, *Well, it's too late now.*

Another thing that bothered me was the fact that we were all family, and family is supposed to support each other. The fact that I did not go back really bothered me because even though I was not graduating, I should have went to support my freedom writer family. I felt really bad about that for a long time because I should have been there, when every single one of my peer's names were called. I should have been there to cheer them on in glory as if we had just won a battle because we did win a battle. Out of all that we went through, we did it. All the pain, struggles, name-calling, people that didn't like us, and we proved them all wrong. They wrote us off and said we were going to be nothing. That we were unreachable. Hell, a lot of us doubted ourselves as I didn't think I was going to live to see sixteen. See, this graduation is more than just us completing twelve years of school; this graduation is our baptism from darkness to light. A group of children who are now becoming young adults. And I missed it. I missed it.

One thing I can definitely take from this as a life experience is that sometimes you have to seize the moment for what it is. Don't let anyone tell you what you can't do. I know if I didn't take no for an answer, I would've heard my name be called in front of thousands at that stadium that day. I would've laughed with my friends and threw my cap in the air and enjoyed the luxury of graduation. If I could do it all over again, I would've fought harder, studied longer, utilized more tutoring, and not let anyone tell me what I couldn't do. Once again, a life lesson given to me by my teacher called life. Every day, I continue to be a student, hoping that one day I can pass this class.

Things were not all bad; I would say that I was probably one of the only people that was able to go to grad night without graduating. I really enjoyed myself and my peers as that was the last night that most of us will all stand together. It's funny how things work out because from that night on, I felt that I would be alone. But for some reason, I realize this would not be the last I would see of Ms. Gruwell and my family, the freedom writers.

Where Do We Go from Here?

Now that everything is all said and done, grad night is gone, and the following day has now appeared. I asked myself, "Where do we go from here?" I didn't know what I was going to do next. Granted, I had a break as when I was very young, I was hit by an eighteen-wheeler truck, and because of that, I had a case settlement that allowed me $10,000 once I turned eighteen. Boy, the price of roadkill nowadays. So you can say, I had a jumpstart on life by being able to purchase a vehicle and a apartment. But I had some unfinished business. Although I was kicked out, labeled as a nobody, and didn't graduate high school, I decided that I had to take my own destiny into my hands and not allow the history of the men in my family of not graduating high school make me its latest victim. I made a decision to go back to adult school to finish off my high school diploma.

I realize that it would take hard work, but I didn't think it should be too hard to finish fifteen credits. I was wrong. To make up those fifteen credits, it seemed like I was trying to make up two years of high school. I did coursework and had tests at the end of every week. It took a lot of sacrifice that I did not believe I had in myself, but I must admit that when you want something so badly, you will do whatever it takes to make that happen. Eventually, it happened: that dream that I had over and over again about graduation, it happened. I was there with a friend of mine that I knew since middle school and we sat in the crowd and listen as the valedictorian gave their speech. I was so overwhelmed as the struggle from elementary school until now played over and over again in my mind like a broken record. I thought about the times I got in trouble and where I could have ended up, had I let society dictate what I was supposed to be and what I was supposed to become.

After the speeches and the musical selections all had ended, thus began the calling of names, they made their way through the As to Fs. Finally, my moment of truth has arrived. I stood up with the rest of the graduates. I followed suit, walking up toward the stage. This time, I looked into the crowd, and my dream of graduation that becomes a nightmare because of the absence of my mother was found to be false. I looked at the seat my mother was supposed to be in and she was there, front and center, smiling with pride along with my sister Patrice. I walked across that stage and shook the principal of the adult school's hand. That day, my dreams came true as my mother witnessed me graduating high school. The count is now complete; we can now say 150 Freedom Writers have graduated. By not graduating, I felt I was not just holding me back but holding back the accuracy of a great story that's being told of 149 students who graduated high school, and now, with my diploma in hand, we are 150 Freedom Writers who graduated high school.

This experience taught me a lot about life as sometimes it's really not about who finishes first or fast, but about who finishes. Because of the motivations in my life, one being my mother, my sister, Ms. Gruwell, and people I encountered in my eighteen years of life, I broke the chain and was the first of the men in the Garrett family to graduate high school. *Wow, life couldn't get any better at this point*, I thought to myself as my mother, sister, and I posed for my graduation picture.

Later, I celebrated, saying, "Yes, I got my diploma." As I danced around my mother with much happiness, my mother then snatches it and says, "It's my diploma." "Why is that?" I replied. She then said, "All the things you took me through, the tough love, trying to make sure you got to school and didn't ditch, motivating you to finish all these years?" I then stopped, thought about it, and clutched my diploma oh so tightly. After replaying my life in a matter of seconds, I handed it over and said, "You're right, Mom…it's your diploma, here you go."

Soul Survivor

As a year or so had quickly passed us by, the freedom writers couldn't help but to see each other again. Most of us were enrolled in college, and it was the old gang back together again. Reminded me of this show I used to watch called *Saved by the Bell,* but the college years. We had all grown from our young high school antics to college students with goals and plans. Along with that, Ms. Gruwell came up with another one of her ideas. Let's start a new class that you can take with me as the teacher and prepare for a trip that is the mother of all trips. Now after she proposed that, I couldn't wrap my mind around what could be bigger than going to Washington or New York. I guess you can say she really outdid herself this time when she dropped the bomb, saying, "Let's take our message of tolerance and hope to Europe." *Wait, Europe!* I thought. Now I know we barely got to Washington with the little jug of change that we raised, now we're trying to go to Europe. But being students of Ms. Gruwell and her "yes we can" mentality, I quickly thought, *Well, guess we will need more jugs then because we're going to Europe.*

We took the classes that Ms. Gruwell presented, and it felt good to see everyone again after a year or so. The freedom writer magic never left. We had a great time, just as we had done in the past. We eventually were able to get the money for Europe. Though triumph was achieved, at the time, tragedy also crept in…one freedom writer didn't make that trip. Just as any fruitful tree that bears fruit, it also has leaves and some do wither and die. I didn't attend his memorial because I knew him and I was burnt out of going to funeral type events. Yet his memory would always live along with me as beyond knowing each other as freedom writers, I met this guy when I was in the first or second grade. He was this little guy compared to me, yet he packed a big stick. He was very mean to me at first, I'll admit, and he seemed like he had asthma as he continually coughed when he talked; it seemed as if he had to always struggle to get a word out.

I would talk to him and he would respond with a smart comment, and I could not understand for the life of me why this kid was so rude. After, he got to know me and I him. We became cool; he actually is very funny. I started to be like a bodyguard for him at school, but then, we graduated from elementary and went on to junior high as I never saw him again until I got into Ms. Gruwell's class. It was so pleasant to meet back up with him again four years down the road. He still suffered from the same ailment that he did when we were in elementary school, but it seemed he had a better hold of it though. When we would come back from our trips to places like Washington, DC, and New York, he would always say, "I'mma go with you guys next time."

Though next time never came in person, I know he was with us in spirit. Before we left for our trip to Europe, I got word from Ms. Gruwell that his frail little body had succumbed to a disease called cystic fibrosis. He was receiving a lung transplant, and his body rejected it. I felt his body was just simply tired of fighting and his soul was now at rest. Ms. Gruwell said that his mother expressed that he did do the three things he wanted to do in life. He got his license, graduated high school, and got the opportunity to go to college as he earned a scholarship. My thoughts are and always will be with him. He taught me a lot as a kid as well as a young adult. No matter what situation you are in, you can always make it better. When someone or something, including your body, tells you that you can't do something, prove them wrong. Through his time on this earth, he had conquered a lot, and for that, I consider my deceased Freedom Writer friend a soul survivor.

Euro Freedom Writers

I cannot believe it. After all that we have been through, we're finally going to Europe. It seemed like it could take so much time to get my passport, but I was able to do so with the help of my newfound mentor in junior-college Mr. Hill. Its funny how he and I met as Ms. Gruwell was the reason for us meeting. I had enrolled at Long Beach City College, and he had become like a big brother/father figure to me. I really admired Mr. Hill as he portrayed everything that I felt I wanted to be as a black man. Anything that I ever needed from advice to maybe a little pocket change to catch the bus, he was right there. So picking up my passport would not have been any different as he took me to the federal building to get my passport.

We went through a lot of hell and high water just so that I can obtain my passport. I had to run around town to find birth certificates as well as Social Security cards. As we flew to Europe, I first recall us going to London. Being in London was so amazing as I saw things that I only saw on television. Like the red phone booths. We got the opportunity to go to Harods, which was the shopping mall in that area actually owned by the late Princess Diana's father. Walking around, I was very amazed by the live manikins that they had there. I must admit that I was very frightened at the fact that I thought they were real manikins until I walked into the store and stared at a manikin that was very beautiful.

Yet as I stared at her with lust in my eyes, she then moved. I jumped, yet I didn't want anyone to know that I was fearful of the live manikin model, so I laughed it off, yet I looked behind me, making sure that she was not following us as we left.

As our day was unwinding, we began to be paired off into partners, and conveniently, I was paired with a couple of roommates that I already hung out with such as my friend Chad and some other freedom writers. My funniest story is when we first got to Europe, we were in our rooms and Chad decided to bring us some entertainment by bringing his video game, the PlayStation. We were all ready to play, yet we didn't know that their electrical system was far different from the US electrical system. So when you go to Europe, you have to have a converter in order to use American products in Europe. Since we were oblivious to that, we were so happy to play the game that Chad then grabbed the plug to the video game, and although the electrical socket looked different, he decided to try and plug the cord to the video game into the wall anyway.

After he plugged it in, he began to tinker with the game and tried to get it to cut on. As he was doing so, one of our friends said, "Hey, Chad, why is your game smoking?" First thing everyone thought was all together at the same time, "Fire!" The alarm began to go off in the hotel, and we began to do all we could to stop the smoke in the mid-fire that was erupting. Although it was the demise of Chad's video game system, we learned a valuable lesson. Bring a converter if you decide to bring any American products into Europe.

Our tour was as so amazing as we saw Big Ben, Buckingham Palace, and I noticed that they had a lot of German cars out there, so I saw Mercedes all over the place. Another thing we got to do was to go to see the play *Grease*. I really love that. From there, I remember going to Poland. I must admit that there are some very beautiful people out in Poland. Things were so different as they ate French fries from McDonald's with mayonnaise, and when I ask for ketchup, I was looked at as if I was nasty. Though one of my favorite movies was *Pulp Fiction,* I had to test out the theory of the quarter pounder. I must say it was definitely true as I looked at the menu and the quarter pounder is definitely called the McRoyal because they don't use the metric system.

As we were going through the different places, there were two filmmakers that were following along, Adriend and Roko Belic. It was interesting as they were there because I felt how it would feel to be on a reality show. The cameras were all around, yet we got so used to the cameras that it became normal. We also began to make friends with the two young film festival winner filmmakers as they were some of the coolest people I could've ever known. Of course, knowing that they had done a film that won awards, my friends Chad, Jones, and I decided to pick their brains to find out what it takes to do exactly what it is that they are doing. I really wanted to know because it seemed like they enjoy their jobs. Seeing them with the smiles that they had every day inspired me to want the same type of happiness within my life. From that time forward, I had made a conscious decision that I would like to do something that I enjoyed for the rest of my life. Once I realized that, I began to seek into what I really liked to do, which was music. Therefore, I made a decision that I would like to start my own record company.

I can see myself now having the most successful record company in the world. With nothing but the best artist that you can find. But more than anything, I realized I would like to be a family man. It would do my heart well to wake up in the morning, pick up my daughter, sat her on my knee as I sit at the computer and enjoy my daughter's company while I'm doing what I love: music. I really appreciate those guys because they surely showed me that once I can make a living doing what I really love, that's when I will never work again. Thank you, Adrian and Roko. I will never forget you.

Anne & Art

O n to our next city, I realize we have now landed into the place that I heard of a few times during my days of smoking and selling drugs, Amsterdam, Holland. One thing I will say about this place is there is so much more to offer than what people think. I really enjoyed the Van Gogh Museum as they displayed all the art from Van Gogh that I had seen in my art book in school that I admired. When I learned about Van Gogh in art class, I did very well in that course because I found a lot of things in him that I seen within myself. Although people may label him as a crazy person, he was an ultimate genius.

I appreciated his outlook on things and the way he painted things as he saw it made me realize that I can do the same thing with my music and rapping to just rap about what I see and how I see it, not caring what others are doing or trying to keep up with anyone else, but just simply doing and being me. Speaking of art, another piece that I was really intrigued by was this art piece called the Pictorama, which was a life-size painting of a beach. I had never seen anything like this. But this painting displayed such genius as it actually looked like I was at the beach.

Since I am on the subject of beaches, we also walked along one and discovered that the norm where we were was far from the norm in the US as we saw people walking around the beach in Speedos or were topless.

I would say that was the ultimate culture clash to me as we believe to be nude is simply absurd, yet to them, wearing clothing to the beach is simply absurd. I must admit being an adolescent boy to see that all around me made me very giddy and giggly, yet as time passed, we began to feel a bit out of place being there with clothes on. I realized they still had homelessness and alcoholism. It didn't seem like too much crime went on out there, yet I do admit we were in the tourist areas. I learned a lot from this place as we walked everywhere, and as I walk the streets of Amsterdam, the architecture was amazing. As time progressed, I began to pay attention to things such as the roads built of stone and the various ways of getting around that they offered. I never would have thought that I would be here.

As I followed the stones in the street in a mesmerized state, the leader of our group yells out here we are. As I stood on the outside, I was simply flawed at what sat before me. The actual attic that I read about in Anne Frank's diary. It looked like a little storefront place. As we entered in, you can simply feel the spirit of Anne Frank. As I walked toward the slim staircase that led to the attic that Anne Frank and her family were huddled in, I began to sulk in my own sorrow of what I could imagine they felt once they realized that they had to go into hiding. As I walked up the narrow, slim stairway, I began to think of how Anne, Otto, Peter, and the rest of the people in the attic must have felt when they went up there, not knowing if they would ever come down again.

As we were in the attic, I can hear the voice in my head of Anne Frank as I looked out the small window that she must have looked out of when she stated that she felt like a bird with its wings clipped. People began to mourn the life of Anne Frank as they also saw what I had seen. It's amazing how one little girl affected so many with something that she never thought the world would see. She wasn't planning on a bestseller or anything like that, but she was just simply keeping a journal. Just like we did with our journals as they later on became the *Freedom Writers' Diary*.

Stand by Me

"Stand by Me," a song I have heard many and many of times as a kid, yet it never had the meaning that it means to me today. We had a good time as we all were able to ride on a boat for a nice lunch as we cruised around the harbor. Thinking that seasickness would set in, I was very worried about getting sick as I have done on many freedom writer trips before. As we got off the bus to walk to the boat, we all posed for a picture. We then entered the boat, and once again as we have done many of times before, we were exposed to pure elegance. This boat was very nice as it seemed like a floating banquet hall. I never saw anything like this before. As we began to move, the motion sickness that I thought I'd experience did not set in. We all had fun as we mingled and music was playing.

Of course, in the spirit of all freedom writer trips, we decided to get together and start freestyling. I'd say a rhyme, then Jones, and by that time, we had other freedom writers that had joined our rap circle as well such as my boy Booker, who is a freedom writer tall, lanky type of guy, very fun-loving, and funny. He could make anyone laugh at nothing. Then there was cook. He was the P. Diddy of the group, great at talking and getting a deal done. Somebody that I know when we do reach our careers, he'll be running the music industry. Then there was Smalls aka Church Boy. I call him Church Boy because to me, he seemed like someone that either grew up in church or had a firm religious upbringing, yet he was very suave with the ladies as well. We all gathered around and brought forth our best rhymes as we had a wonderful time. A time in which I wish I immortalized it with video.

Music outside of our rap circle began to play and the festivities began. Anytime the freedom writers get together, it's a party. We were dancing and rocking along with the boat. This is another element of the freedom writer magic. One in which would bring the most shy person out of their shell to have a good time. We did every dance from the macarena to the moonwalk. As we danced, it became infectious as others that were on the boat but not in our party decided to join in as well. Talk about wild and crazy, My excitement was that of a child that had his first trip to Disneyland. I appreciated this experience as a moment in time that I could never have erased from my memory because it was a time just like the others as a freedom writer when I was allowed to just be me. As the music as well as the party began to unwind, we all gathered together and Jones began the sing-along.

"When the night…has come." He began the words to the song "Stand by Me," and at that time, it was so fitting as I looked to my left and I saw a Caucasian freedom writer, then I looked to my right and saw a punk rocker freedom writer, then looked across from me and saw my teacher that I had now had for over three years, Ms. Gruwell. But it seemed like she was crying. I wondered why she was crying, but as I began to sing more lyrics to the song "Stand by Me," I began to sob a bit myself because the more we sang, the more things played back in my mind. Like when I first met Jones about to fight him and now we're really good friends, then I looked at Chad and thought to myself how great it felt to have a close friend that's like a brother. Then I watched Cook as he was smiling and singing along, then it hit me. This was one time out of many since being a freedom writer that we all were in the same room, smiling at the same time, which brought me back to who was in front of me. Ms Gruwell. The woman that has been like a mother to me since she met me. A woman that didn't care if I was white, black, or red with green polka dots on my back. She loved me for me, and at that moment, I realized that the tear I saw fall down her face was a tear of joy.

She was looking at all of us just as I was looking at her, yet she was as a proud parent to see all of us that made it. I didn't think I'd see sixteen and she knew that, and I made it past sixteen and not just that but we are in Europe. A place that my parents or some people that have been world heroes have never been. I'm so taken by all of this, I forgot that we were in the middle of singing, yet I darted across from me to give Ms. Gruwell something that I had wanted to give her since our trip to Europe started. On my way across to her, I began to think of the times when school was out and over with; she could have left us. She could have said, "Okay, baby birdies, you are out the nest, now fly," like so many of our parents had done. But she didn't do that, she stayed. She saw us through and truly stood by me, and in the words of my mother, she would always say,

"Give me my flowers while I am alive," meaning pay respect and homage while the person is still with us. I didn't have any money or anything significant to give her, so I gave her the best thing that I knew showed my emotions, something that I'd asked my mother for time and time again. A hug.

Am I My Brother's Keeper?

My brother and I have not had the best relationship in the world, yet I learned a lot from him. You can call it bittersweet as he was there for a lot of my problems, run-ins with the law, as well as advice I needed at the time that may not have been the best advice, yet he made himself available when he could to answer and be there. From the quickly grown fame of our book, it made it possible for me to travel and do things that I had never thought I would do such as having a speaking engagement in Memphis, Tennessee, and having the opportunity to meet and spend time with my sister Edie that I never knew I had until I was a teenager. Since I was a little kid, my brother Edward and I were like twins. We were inseparable yet couldn't stand each other. Sometimes, we would fight as if we were each other's arch nemesis, then at other times, we would talk and hang out with each other like best friends.

I personally think it was because he always thought that since our dad wasn't really in our lives that he had to be that father figure. I would say that in some part, he was right, but in being a father figure, he had to set a fatherly example. We had a lot of issues yet a couple that was most memorable all resorted from the times that we fought each other because I honestly felt that when I fought him that I was fighting for my life. As much as he said that he was not trying to hurt me, I thought different. I loved my brother unconditionally, yet we would always go through things that made me want to feel less and less for him. I couldn't stop my love for my brother because we were blood, and for some reason, that caused me to continue to allow him to take advantage of my love and kindness.

I had come to terms after our last fight that I was going to give up on him. Many times, I had spoken with family members about how I was being treated, just seeking advice, and people beyond my family all reminded me that I can continue to love him, yet love him from a distance. I took that advice and it seemed to work. My brother began to call me from time to time, and he began to do more than what I thought he would do as he promised when he was in jail that once he got out that he was going to do better. I heard that song and dance before, and I had refused to fall into that trap. I must admit that he was right. When he got out of jail, he got himself a girlfriend. Got custody of his sons and moved to Tennessee with his newly built family. I must admit that I was proud of him because he had come a long way.

One night, I remember a call from him, and he was trying to figure out something about his computer. He called and I answered his question, yet I could hear him and his girlfriend arguing in the background. I began to think maybe he hasn't changed because of some of the things being said, yet I didn't know the situation and began to judge off the merit and broken rapport that he previously built with me. All I could do is just pray he doesn't make the wrong decisions and continue about my day. Yet when I shared with him how to fix his computer, he was very happy, and the last thing I heard before he hung up the phone was "That's my little bro, he knows everything…I knew he could do it."

I must admit it put a smile on my face, and I was happy that he was happy. As I was on tour doing a speaking engagement in a juvenile facility, I began to share with the guys that were locked up my story, and as I looked at their faces, I thought of the faces of my brother's kids. My nephews and nieces, as I panned across the room, I saw a young man that actually reminded me of my brother, and it hurt my heart as it reminded me of how history repeats itself as my father went to prison and then my brother. Plus with my run-ins with the law, it seemed that my life was inevitable to be headed down the wrong path, yet at that moment, I realized that I was there in jail but to help this time and it made me very happy.

After the speaking engagement, we all went to go eat and debrief on the day and how it went at the detention center. My phone rang and it was my brother. I looked at it and thought to myself that its not important and put my phone away. It began to vibrate over and over again, meaning that he continued to try and contact me, and still, I didn't answer. One of my biggest dreams was to make it in the entertainment industry and have my brother right there by my side when I did it. Yet just like other dreams, that one too had come to an end as a few days later, I received a phone call that my brother died of a brain aneurysm. Although I'm not the cause of his death, I feel so indebted and responsible for it.

Who knows what he was calling me for, and now, I will never know. I fight every day with the thoughts of maybe I could have done or said something to save him and that would have allowed me to have my brother today. Yet through the sense of responsibility, I do sit back and ask myself, "Am I my brother's keeper?"

Welcome to Hollywood

G litz and glamour, fame and fortune is what most people crave in Hollywood, or so I thought. Yet I realized that it all comes down to money. After all we had done as freedom writers, we had never thought that we would encounter the inevitable as we were all contacted on the freedom writer bat phone to meet up as a big announcement was going to take place. We went to the location, and on my way into the parking lot of the place we all agreed to meet, I saw this short guy walking up to the car from a distance. The closer he got the more familiar he seemed.

Oh snap…it's the dude that played the penguin in *Batman*. Though he was one of my favorite actors from *One Flew over the Cuckoo's Nest*, *Batman*, *Twins*, and *Junior*, etc. I could not remember his name until he introduced himself. "Hi, I'm Danny…Danny Devito," he said. *Yes, yes that's it*. I was so star struck I couldn't remember his name. As we entered the place, I saw a lot of freedom writers that I had not seen in years including my old friend Jones that had arrived with a kid and wife. Other freedom writers had shown up and still looked the same; granted, we have been out of high school now for at least nine years. So it was very interesting to find out who had kids, who's gotten married, and who has not. Fortunately, I'm glad I'm not married and probably never will.

As everyone gathered together, Ms. Gruwell began to introduce everyone that was involved with this announcement. Be it that Mr. Devito was involved, I knew it had something to do with a movie or maybe a documentary. I grew more and more excited. The anticipation built as they continued to talk about everything but the announcement. After everyone was formally introduced, the moment of truth had now arrived, and the announcement was made just like the announcement we received of having a book deal. She said that we have agreed to a deal with Paramount Pictures as they are going to make a movie about the freedom writers. Everyone was so excited, including me. I was overwhelmed with the wonder to who will play me as a character in the movie. I got to sit down with the director, Richard Lagravenese and he asked me various questions of how I do certain things as to how I talk, how I walk, how I would show various facial expressions or reactions to certain things. When asked about the name that I'd like my character to have, I picked "Marcus," the legal name of my friend Smurf, who had shot himself in front of me. This was the first script I had ever read. I was thoroughly pleased as I read it. I could see the movie playing in my head. I will say the movie magic process is very lengthy yet satisfying. I never got to work with such pleasant people. I got to meet and hang out with a lot of people because of the *Freedom Writer* movie on set such as Hilary Swank, singer Mario, and others. Through their casting, I felt they matched it right on as the character based on me;

Marcus was played by this new up and coming actor named Jason Finn.

Alongside the rest of the cast, Jason was one of the coolest guys. He empathized with my personal story and could play the role of me so well because all he had to do was take from his own life. One thing I realized is that we all go through a lot of the same things. Though I was already part of the movie with Marcus being based on me and in the movie as a featured extra as well, it didn't seem enough as I was invited to audition by sending them a demo tape of my music. From that point on, things were never the same. I had received a phone call that my music has been picked up to be part of the movie soundtrack. I had submitted a few songs, but the one picked up was a song called "Change" that I co-wrote with my friends and fellow songwriters Kashaun Johnson and Intan Sebastian.

I also had got the opportunity to go into the studio with hit producer Will.i.am and rapper Common. Listening and being a fan of Common was a dream come true to finally be in a position like that. I bounced back and forth from the studio I was recording in Hollywood and their studio that they were recording in. From that day forward, I realized that I wanted to do this every day of my life. When the star struck-ness died down, it was straight to work as we created and recorded "Change" and went on set to finish shooting the movie. I was finally exposed to movie magic and what it was really all about. It was a project that anyone especially the writer and director treats as its baby, and when you reveal your baby to the world, you want people to see it as that precious work of timeless art. Because of that, the freedom writers held and attended multiple screenings to see what people thought of the movie. Once the process was done, the movie was green lighted (*Okayed*) to be released.

While I was on the ultimate high of the movie and my song being released. I had to go back to the reality of working a regular job. The place I worked at had a bus stop directly across the street that displayed the *Freedom Writers* movie as a billboard. I would tell everyone about it and that I was part of it, but they wouldn't believe me. They didn't even believe I was a freedom writer…funny. I wouldn't care if they believed me or not though because by the end of 2007, they will know my name.

Make Her Proud

My mother and I have been through many ups and downs, yet I recognize that she will always be my mother and that she is the best thing I have in my life. I can remember the many times I woke up as a kid and saw my mother, early in the morning, praying for me. She prayed with all her might that God would protect me and keep me from being locked up or killed. I remember like it was yesterday. Neither of us had too much faith that I would live to see sixteen at the time that I was in high school because it seemed that everywhere I went, trouble followed. As if death was around every corner.

I dealt with it through just accepting it. As I got older, people who heard my story would ask me how I dealt with the idea of death and dying. I would think about it for a minute and reply, "See, being poor, black, and living in the ghetto was kind of like a disease that I was born with, sort of like AIDS or cancer." One of the most memorable moments of my mother and I is one when my mother and I were on our way to the Freedom Writers Foundation to get on a charter bus to go to the premiere of our movie *Freedom Writers*. I couldn't believe it. We were actually on our way to see our movie. On the bus, the same camaraderie we felt in room 203 began to emerge as we talked and told jokes. Although I really enjoyed myself, I realized things were definitely different now—we weren't kids anymore. No rapping,

211

or singing just the bus ride; God, I miss Jones. We were the people we had dreaded becoming as kids; we were now hardworking, law-abiding, taxpaying adults.

I glanced at my mom and I saw a proud-parent-type smile on her face. As I was looking at her, I reflected on the days when I was young and would tell my mom, "One day, I'm going to be a star and people will know my name." As we approached the theater, all we could see were flashing lights, red carpet, pandemonium, and paparazzi. But most important, we saw the fans, people who really appreciated our story and struggles. As we stepped off the bus, we were happily greeted by the crowds. I was happier to see them though. As we walked into the movie theater, for some reason, I got more and more nervous. I knew I wasn't the director or the producer of the film, but part of it was my story, and I was worried about what people would think, especially my mother.

As the movie played, the character based on me appeared on the screen and people in the theater started to say my name, as if I were somebody they had always known. It was such a wonderful feeling because people actually connected to my story. It was so amazing to see my character come alive on the big screen. He walked like me, acted like me, and even stayed to himself like me. All I could think was wow. At one point, there was a scene in which my character returned home to his mother after convincing her he had made a positive change in his life. It was so amazing to see that scene and so surreal to something that actually happened in my life reenacted like that.

All I could think about was where I would have been if my mother had not taken me back into her home that night and I had just remained homeless. Where would I have been? What would I have done? Then I looked over at my closest friend Chad and his mom, and I remembered his story of homelessness and the many times I stayed with them at their house. After what they had been through, they would never want anyone else on the street. I smiled and knew I would have been all right.

As people clapped, I looked at my mother, and it seemed as if that scene in which my character came back home had taken her back to that specific time in our lives, just as it had done for me. I suddenly felt the bond that my mother and I have had since birth. It may have been hidden at times, such as on the day she kicked me out of the house, but I realized our mother-son bond had never been broken. When we walked out of the theater, people were asking me for hugs, autographs, and to answer their questions. Some people even wanted to give my mother a hug because she had given me a second chance.

While I was posing for pictures with other freedom writers and signing autographs for people who were really moved by the movie, I looked to the side and saw my mom with that same proud parent smile that she had given me on the bus. This time when I saw her smiling at me, I realized that I wanted to continue to put that smile on her face for the rest of my life.

Mirror, Mirror

As the seasons grew, so did life. Three years later, my mother died of cancer. I felt I lost my best friend, my counselor, and most of all, my mother. I was devastated and felt a pain that I had not felt in a while. I found myself in the mirror preparing for her funeral. I didn't see my mother's death just as a loss of a family member or a friend but also the loss of myself. I never thought my mother would leave me like this. The pain seemed too much to bear. I thought of how much I didn't want to live anymore and the fact that I don't have both parents until a small voice inside reminded me that although my mother died and I felt I needed her, there is a little girl that was born a couple of months ago named Sarye that needed me more.

From that day forward, I realized that I went through my whole life looking for this man to be in my life. A guy that would play with his kids, show up at all the events, be the loudest one in the stands when his kids graduate and make a conscious decision to not do drugs. Looking in that same mirror as a tear escaped my right eye, I realized for the first time, that man for which I was seeking for all my life was ME. Life trained me to be the man that my kids needed as my family grew during the following year. I had another little girl name Aaliyah. After I got married on November 11, 2011, and committed to my girlfriend of three years, Jamia, and made her my wife.

On the day of my wedding, I had a moment of silence for my mother as part of the wedding ceremony.

I realized that though my mother was not present, her presence was definitely felt as my sister Patrice; that helped raised me was part of the festivities of my wedding. While reciting my vows, I saw a familiar face. That of someone that promised she would be a mother figure when I needed it most, Ms. Gruwell. My life had turned for the better. I know I had failed my mother many times, but this time, I know she was proud of me. When asked do I take my wife's hand in marriage, I looked at my sister, my two daughters, Ms. Gruwell, and back at the beautiful face of my wife and eagerly said, "I do."

Afterthoughts

In my lifetime, I have seen a lot of things, things that some relate to, and other things that folks would say, "Wow how did you make it through that?" Honestly, if I had to sum it up in one word, my answer would be, "Faith." My faith has been the story of my whole life. It took faith for me to be born with jaundice and meningitis, although my mother's tubes were tied and the doctor saying that my mother and I may not make it through the night, faith saw us through. It took faith for my mother to not abort me as a baby and have me at the age of thirty-six. It took faith for me to make it to age sixteen, twenty-one, then twenty-five, and now thirty, with my next milestone being thirty-five. It took faith for Ms. Gruwell to see that we were going to be better than what we even thought of ourselves. It took the faith of us to step out and even allow her to help us. It took the faith of me to continue to go to school even though I was homeless, and most of all, it took faith for me to grow up in the places I grew up in and just simply survive.

That is what my story is about—survival. That's what my life is about—surviving. Are you a survivor? I am a firm believer that if you live by the sword, you die by the sword, and dealing with the street life, the sword was the only thing that governed the streets; therefore, that's how I lived. I've had over thirty-five friends and family members die because of drugs and violence, and I felt that I wasn't any different from them. A lot of people ask if I have any regrets to the way that I lived my life or the things I went through and I would answer, saying, "No" because it made me the person that I am today. But as of lately, I would have to change my answer. I wish I had lived life a little more, loved a little more, and listened to my mother a lot more than I actually did.

I have seen a lot of crazy things from the drug game to death, and I realized that I wasn't meant for any of it. To this day as an adult in his thirties, I still have nightmares and wake up with cold sweats, panic, anxiety attacks because of the things I encountered as a kid and a teenager. I hope one day to channel all that has inspired me to become a man that possesses the wisdom of Dean Kinsey, the business know how of Mr. John Tu, the strength of my mother, Marie Garrett, the courage of Miep Gies, the happiness of Roko and Adrien Belic, the concern and love of Don Parris, the smarts of my sister Patrice Perkins, the kindness of my brother-in-law Johnny Perkins, the fatherhood of my Uncle Larry, and continue the legacy of Erin Gruwell and The Freedom Writers, offering hope and tolerance throughout the world.

So far, I realize that life is what we make it. The key honestly lay within our minds and hearts. Yet it is up to us to unlock and walk through the door of preparedness that leads to our windows of opportunity. Though I have had many adversities and obstacles, I realize that a lot of the time, I have been in my own way. If you want to see who is stopping you from doing what you dream, go look in the mirror and tell that person, "No more." No more will you stop me from following my dream.

No more will you say, I will not get out of jail. No more will you say, I can't teach 150 students, teach them for over three years, and take them on field trips to Washington, DC, New York, or Europe. I realize that life is definitely a game. Some win and some lose, but how you play the game is what defines who we are as an individual. As much as I want to be the richest man alive, I realize that I can contribute to that dream, but not control it.

What I can control is the hundreds of thousands of people I have shared my story with and the millions more in which I will share my story, and out of millions, one of you will take this baton of tolerance and hope, just as Miep had done for me, and live out your dreams and fulfill your goals. Upon that, I build my success. My experiences made me who I am; therefore, I share with you my memoirs, my experiences, and my diary of a freedom writer so that you too may encounter "The Experience."

Darrius and mommie

Darrius and mommie

Darrius and first daughter Sarye

Garrett Family

married man walking

Darrius' three daughters

Darrius signing books

Darius with inspired students from Oregon

Printed in Great Britain
by Amazon.co.uk, Ltd.,
Marston Gate.